THE CHOICE CALLED *ATHEISM*

THE CHOICE CALLED *ATHEISM*

Orlo Strunk, Jr.

ABINGDON PRESS Ⓐ NASHVILLE & NEW YORK

THE CHOICE CALLED ATHEISM

Copyright © 1968 by Abingdon Press

Library of Congress Catalog Card Number: 68-25364

Scripture quotations noted RSV are from the Revised
Standard Version of the Bible, copyrighted 1946 and
1952 by the Division of Christian Education, National
Council of Churches, and are used by permission.

Scripture quotations noted NEB are from the New
English Bible, New Testament. © the Delegates of the
Oxford University Press and the Syndics of the Cambridge
University Press 1961. Reprinted by permission.

The excerpts from *Atheism in Our Time* by Ignace Lepp
are reprinted with permission of The Macmillan Company. © The Macmillan Company 1963.

SET UP, PRINTED, AND BOUND BY THE
PARTHENON PRESS, AT NASHVILLE,
TENNESSEE, UNITED STATES OF AMERICA

To

Laura Louise

and

John Christopher

*Only two of the millions of children
on this earth who make the search
for a more understanding world an
absolute necessity*

PREFACE

Why a book on atheism?

At a time when spiritual plurality is at a high point, it is important that Christian laymen make every effort possible to understand the choices of world views facing mankind. Atheism, I believe, has never been quite so live an option as it is today. The fact that over one third of mankind presently lives under the sway of a regime which accepts atheism as its official spiritual stand is in itself a stark reminder of the significance of the topic. But equally sobering is the fact that practically every major world view, including Christianity itself, harbors splinter groups which hold atheism as their battle flag.

Indeed, I am convinced that atheism in any one of its sundry forms is not only a live option, but it can be, and often is, an exceptionally appealing choice in a world drenched in the blood of millions of innocent victims who appear to be little more than the chattel of a blind and irresponsible set of impersonal forces.

No longer is it legitimately possible for the Christian to claim with the Old Testament psalmster, "The fool says in his heart, 'There is no God.'" Such a judgment is not only inaccurate, it is a manifest oversimplification. Some of the greatest minds of human history have claimed atheism as a reasonable option. They were not, are not, fools!

Nor is it possible for the contemporary Christian to dismiss atheism as an immoral stance quite without human integrity. Indeed, the very opposite can be argued; it would be exceedingly difficult to determine who has executed more atrocities on humanity— organized believers or atheistic activists. Certainly history, if it is read soberly and with compassion, can show us splendidly moral men who have held to atheism as a proper and reasonable position. The fact is that some of the strongest contemporary arguments *for* atheism are rooted in a profound desire to better the lot of mankind.

These traditional answers to atheism, along with some others to be considered in this volume, simply do not come up to the standard set for us by our Lord Jesus Christ. As Pascal so aptly put it, "The greatest of Christian truths is the love of truth." Modern Christians, and especially modern Christian laymen, must face contemporary atheism in a realistic and intelligent fashion if they are to take seriously their Lord's claim that the truth will set us free. To dismiss another man's faith in a cold and indifferent way, even and especially if that "faith" takes the form of unbelief, is to be something considerably less than Christian.

Instead, the Christian layman has the obligation to try to understand all those who oppose or are indifferent to his faith. Though this little book is certainly not a definitive statement on contemporary atheism and therefore does not provide the layman with all the understanding he ought to have on this subject, it does present him with an introductory outline of information and opinion which should prove helpful to him in his continuous commitment to the search for meaning in the contemporary world.

My aim in this volume, then, becomes a rather direct and simple one: *I wish only to present introductory information on that spiritual option called atheism and to set forth such information in a way which will be meaningful and helpful to Christian laymen.*

I cannot recall ever having written a book or an article in which the intended reader was so firmly held in mind throughout the writing process. I have seen this reader before me at every turn, or, perhaps more appropriately, at the end of every sentence and in the midst of every paragraph. And on more than one occasion this intended reader has seemed to speak to me, to respond to my ideas, and to enter into the argument. There have even been times when he has fallen asleep in the midst of my discussion. At such moments I have gone back and erased my words only to rewrite them in a way which might possibly cause him to sit up and take notice.

I trust, however, that whenever I have done such rephrasing I have not done it with my tongue in my cheek, determined to keep my reader awake and with me at any cost; but, instead, I have tried again in such a way that what I wished to say would take on an immediacy, a personal importance, which he could not afford to ignore. For, as I have already said, I am convinced that contemporary atheism is one of the most crucial spiritual options available to man today, and especially to my intended reader, the "typical" Christian layman!

And just who is this "typical" Christian layman?

Certainly I shall have to admit that my imagined reader is something of a phantom. I've met him, I'm sure, at various laymen's institutes, in several church school classes, at many annual denominational conferences, during not a few church financial campaigns, and in front of scores of rural churches on Sunday morning. Also, I have met him on planes and trains, in places of business, and even in the grandstands of baseball parks! Some of the younger ones, I have met on beaches, the front steps of educational plants, and in snack bars.

Though this layman is a variety of persons, he has one single trait which he shares with all his fellow laymen: *he is convinced, either vaguely or sharply, that what a man believes is, over the long haul, an important ingredient of life*. He may not always know exactly how certain behavior comes about, but he does know that in some way the picture of the world men carry around in their heads is a matter of extreme importance.

One of the major joys of writing a book's preface is the opportunity it gives to record the many debts of gratitude which I owe in the course of the preparation of a book. Unlike many *readers* of books, as a *writer* of books, I do not consider lightly this practice of acknowledging debts. Indeed, to me it is one of the high points in this business of book writing, for it never ceases to amaze me how very helpful and kind most people are when it comes to assisting me in my struggles with a stubborn manuscript!

I especially thank Mr. Raymond W. Kiser, for many years an active Christian layman, for reading the first draft of the manuscript and for offering his opinions and suggestions. And Dr. Catherine Gunsalus gave me invaluable bibliographical assistance in the early stages of writing, as did the entire library staff at West Virginia Wesleyan College, my teaching institution.

I owe a special debt to my secretary, Mrs. Ina Maye Bean, who typed and retyped the manuscript and assisted in preparing the index. Without her willingness to work beyond the ordinary assignments of a college dean's secretary, I would never have been able to hold to my writing schedule.

My wife, Mary Louise, herself an active laywoman in the local church and keenly aware of many of the problems posed in this volume, more than once pulled me up short whenever I started sounding like a college professor; for this, and for graciously freeing me from the typical wifely expectation that a husband should be a handyman around the house, I record publicly my honest appreciation.

Finally, I must express my profound gratitude to the many students, especially those in my course in the psychology of religion, who have been willing to discuss the role of religion in our contemporary society. Their youthful stance and critical appraisals have often kept me from closing an issue before it was ready to be closed.

ORLO STRUNK, JR.

West Virginia Wesleyan College

CONTENTS

PART I

The Roots of Atheism

1. Who Is an Atheist?

---

*All those who possess in its pure state the love of
their neighbour and the acceptance of the order of
the world, including affliction—all those, even
should they live and die to all appearances atheists,
are surely saved.*

—Simone Weil

*The atheist staring from his attic window is often
nearer to God than the believer caught up in his
own false image of God.*

—Martin Buber

Concerned over the perennial problem of
the great gap between man's assertions and his acts,
Jesus once reminded his followers of a disquieting
fact. He said, "Not everyone who calls me 'Lord,
Lord' will enter the kingdom of Heaven" (Matt.
7:21 NEB). Though there are many lessons to be
learned from this bit of scripture, certainly one is that
not everything is what it appears to be. More directly,
not everyone is precisely what he claims he is. There
always have been those Christians who on occasion
cry "Lord, Lord" but who demonstrate no meaningful

understanding of their Lord's expectations for their lives. Such people—and these include all of us at some time or other—never really succeed in making their *theology* their *psychology*. The gap between their belief claims and their behavior is simply too wide.

But the opposite kind of gap can also exist. Not all who cry, "God is dead!" are atheists, and not all who argue, "There is no God!" are unbelievers. Even more important, not all who are violently branded "atheist" are far from a living God.

Atheism, like belief, must be seen in context. And contemporary atheism—far more complex than much of classical atheism—especially needs our careful attention. Though it is true, as we shall sense later, that many modern writers on the subject of atheism end up by making atheists appear believers and believers atheists, we cannot let this tendency force us into oversimplifying the problem of identifying atheism. At least we have a responsibility to come to some general understanding of what is meant by atheism as we view the term in this study. Such will be the primary aim of this chapter.

The Many Meanings of Atheism

I once overheard two Chicago cab drivers arguing over a parking place. The parking place was large enough for one car only, but both taxis were half-parked and neither driver would give. The one driver insisted that he had got there first. The second driver argued that he parked in this particular space every Thursday morning to wait for an elderly lady who came from Mass; he insisted that the old lady wanted him to drive her home. But the first driver told him to circle the block and search for his fare. Finally, in heated exasperation, the second driver tore away from the curb with the shout, "Go to hell, you damn atheist!"

Less than an hour later I listened to a Catholic sister deliver a paper on the place of Mariology in the Christian faith. At one point she said, "Atheism really means that we ought to live in relation to our fellow-men, not to God. In this sense the atheist is one who puts all his trust and love in his brothers of this world."

Though I never had the chance to examine in detail either the cab driver's or the nun's meaning of atheism, I suppose they meant different things. It is true of course, that a word may have different levels of usage. These sentences by Theodore Bernstein make this point wonderfully well:

The recognition that there are levels of usage is, of course, nothing new; we have always known that different elements of the population employ different kinds of language. . . . Although levels of usage have always been recognized, what is new in the contemporary world is the equal blessing bestowed on all of them. And implicit in that blind blessing is a reluctance to hurt anyone's feelings or to make him feel inferior. This attitude is puzzling. There are more poor fiddlers than good ones, but no one hesitates to say that there is such a thing as good violin playing. There are more golfers who play in the nineties and above than play in the seventies, but no one hesitates to say that there is a correct way to play out of a sandtrap or a correct club to use on the green. There are more do-it-yourself carpenters who bungle than there are competent professionals, but no one hesitates to say that there is a right way to fashion a tenon and mortise and a wrong way. In none of these fields do ideas of right and wrong seem to be injurious. In language alone are the bunglers blessed.[1]

We can gather from this that the uses we put words to ought to be seen as a kind of stewardship. Though our contemporary world tends to treat words lightly and imprecisely, the Christian has the obligation to take words very seriously. He ought never let himself become a blessed bungler, if he can help it.

The word "atheism," therefore, must hold our attention for a time, even if such an effort may at first seem painful and decidedly academic. Such an excursion is not only an obligation we inherit as Christians, it is also a responsibility we owe to our brothers who call themselves atheists.

[1] *The Careful Writer* (New York: Atheneum, 1965), pp. xiii-xiv.

If we start on the common ground floor, we find such definitions of atheism as these:

Disbelief in, or denial of, the existence of a supreme being.

Disbelief in the existence of a God or supreme being.

Denial that there is any God, no matter in what sense "God" be defined.

Belief that there is no God.

These sample definitions are what we might call *literal renderings*. We might wish to nod and say, "Okay, these I understand. Now let's let well enough alone!" These literal renderings seem simple enough. But, really, if we insist on accepting this one level of usage, we will easily qualify as word bunglers—especially if we take seriously the fact that many thinkers, both ancient and modern, mean something considerably more than what these literal definitions of atheism seem to say.

For example, some philosophers have called "atheist" those people who do not believe in a *personal* God; in this sense atheism means "not theistic." Or there have been those, such as the French mystic quoted at the head of this chapter, who call themselves atheists because they do not believe in God's *existence* (in the sense that a chair or this book exists) though they are convinced of the *reality* of God. Other atheists claim that their stance really means that they prefer to live fully in relation to their fellowmen rather than to God; they prefer *anthropology* (the science of man and mankind) to *theology* (the science of divine things).

Though we may shake our heads over what may appear to be the scholars' balderdash, if we keep in mind that such extensions of a word frequently stem from an honest attempt to describe a person's experience, we might not be so quick to shake off these less literal meanings. Also, if we recognize the importance of atheism in today's world, we might coax forth greater patience in the quest for a more profound understanding of the term "atheism."

On this latter point one of the most articulate interpreters of contemporary atheism recently wrote: "Atheism has become the lot, if not of the majority of our contemporaries, at least of a very high proportion of them, and it tends to become the common norm of human society. Moreover, present-day atheism declares itself to be not only the denial of a specific religion but of all gods; it claims that man and the universe have absolute autonomy. It holds all religious belief to be the enemy of reason, which is implicitly viewed as the sole criterion of truth." [2]

Such a sober evaluation of contemporary atheism requires the Christian's best thinking, to say the least. Though his flesh may resist this hard responsibility, his love of truth will need to prevail.

[2] Ignace Lepp, "The Church and Atheists," *Commonweal* (October 16, 1964), p. 89.

ATHEISM IN MAN'S HISTORY

We twentieth-century Christians often forget that
one of the most frequent and violent accusations cast
at early Christians was "Atheists!" Because the members of the primitive church did not acknowledge the
official state gods, they were branded as atheists by
the central government. This simple historical fact
can help us see two important aspects of atheism: first,
it is not something new, and second, its meaning takes on various shades with the changing of the
centuries.

The fact that atheism is an old stance ought to be
appreciated by us. The Old Testament contains pas-
sages which point toward the presence of unbelievers.
Perhaps the most famous reference is the beginning
of the fourteenth psalm:

> The fool says in his heart, "There is no God."
> They are corrupt, they do abominable deeds,
> there is none that does good. (RSV)

Though biblical scholars frequently point out that
the Hebrew people did not submit philosophical
arguments over the question of God's existence, it
appears that there were exceptions and that at least
a few people denied God if only in their hearts. The
fact would seem to be that the belief in a God is not
something that comes naturally. Certainly there is no
instinct to believe in a personal God as some scholars

once argued. As far as we can tell, the atheistic stance has been present in every epoch of man's history.

It also seems to be true that frequently those who have been called atheists were products of misunderstanding or were viewed in narrow contexts. The early Christians believed in a God, but he was not the God of the official government of the day.

Socrates, the Greek philosopher born nearly five hundred years before Christ, was accused of atheism by his antagonist, Meletus, but by sheer logic alone this great teacher demonstrated the falseness of Meletus' charges.

Such historic events, along with the apparent nature of atheism in the past, may further be illustrated by reference to Martin Luther's answer to the question of what it means to have a God. The Father of the Reformation once observed that God is what we hang our heart on. It may be money or power or science or the state or any one of a thousand things. In each case, however, we depend on it and give our final allegiance to it. In this sense atheism is impossible because everyone hangs his heart on at least one thing.

Though such an argument appears sound enough, it does not greatly help us to understand the atheist, and in a sense it is an unfair position to those who consciously claim to be atheists even though they may be dedicated to the state or some other institution. Later we shall look closer at this argument and treat it in the discussion dealing with idols. It is

24

mentioned here only to show that throughout man's spiritual history atheism has not only appeared in its literal meaning, but in a context as extensive and complex as we shall find it in the contemporary world.

ATHEISM AND AGNOSTICISM

Part of the confusion found in any attempt to find the meaning of the term "atheism" stems from that spiritual position which has come to be called agnosticism. In a literal sense agnosticism is the theory of knowledge which claims that it is impossible for man to attain knowledge, or from the point of concern of the subject matter of this book, the theory of religious knowledge which says that it is impossible for man to attain knowledge of God.

But once again the level of usage of words must make us cautious. It is one thing to say "I don't know" and something quite different to say "I cannot know." Or perhaps the even more stark: "No one can know!"

In our scientific day agnosticism is an appealing and tempting position. And it is surely true that there are many more agnostics in the world than there are atheists. For agnosticism is an open-ended system which frequently gives the impression of genuine humility. After all, who among us can stand in the midst of this world, look clear-eyed into its turmoil and confusion, and claim, "Yes, I know what it is all about"? Such a one does not attract us, does he?

On the other hand, read these words from a contemporary agnostic:

To accept the agnostic position does not mean that one must defend all agnostics, any more than to accept Catholicism one must defend the personal characters of popes Sixtus IV and Alexander VI. We all enjoy characterizing positions that we do not like in terms of their disreputable exponents. Agnosticism as a final dogma may well invite sneers. It is only a stimulus to search, which accepting any dogma as final is not. The true agnostic is not interested in whether man can "even" know the truth as a whole. He sees little prospect of such an end, but is agnostic on that also. What he wants is to find out a little more than he knows now, and this the man who really thinks that he has the final answers cannot understand. Far from being a negative position, it is the greatest positive stimulus man has.[3]

These words surely draw us to the writer. In these difficult days of complex problems, humility becomes a strong and necessary virtue. In a sense only the fool can thump his chest and say, "I know! I know!" And when "I don't know" is said in sincere compassion, we are bound to be drawn to it. But agnosticism too must be examined minutely. Not all who claim agnosticism are guided by a spirit of searching and humility.

[3] Edwin R. Goodenough, *The Psychology of Religious Experiences* (New York: Basic Books, 1965), p. 182.

In its religious claims it, like much contemporary atheism, says that God is not apparent; evil and suffering are. Unlike atheism, which frequently asserts that God is absent or dead, it says, "We simply do not know whether or not God is and acts."

At this point our attention to agnosticism is to recognize it as a legitimate spiritual option—but not to be confused with atheism. Atheism *does* claim to know, and it therefore presents the Christian with an entirely different set of propositions.

ATHEISM AND ANTITHEISM

If atheism and agnosticism are to be recognized as being essentially different, it must also be seen that atheism and antitheism are cut in different patterns though from the same cloth. To understand this distinction and this affinity, we might start with these rather direct words from the pen of the scholar Etienne Borne:

Atheism, the deliberate, definite, dogmatic denial of the existence of God, and specifically of the God of the religious consciousness, is not satisfied with approximate or relative truth, but claims to see the ins and outs of the game quite clearly: being the absolute denial of the Absolute, atheism must make itself safe from the attacks of doubt. God is dead, to use Nietzsche's words, for he is a human invention, and shares the precariousness which is the lot of all that is "human, all too human." Transcendence and mystery are dismissed as mistakes, distorted ideas produced by the imagination, which in man's earliest history made a fantastic and illusory world.[4]

The key words in this dramatic assertion are *transcendence* and *mystery*. Though Borne's prose is perhaps too direct and comprehensive for us at this point in our study, the fact is clearly made: atheism, especially contemporary atheism, frequently counts transcendence and mystery as man-made mistakes. Such an assertion invariably is an attack on *theism*—the belief in a God who has created man and the world and who *cares* for them.

The fact is, as we shall see in later chapters, much of contemporary atheism is not an attack on religion as such but on Christianity, which has been and remains essentially theistic. Modern atheism is set on rooting out the idea of God from all human experience; it attempts to deny God's transcendence and his movement in history. As a result much atheism is really antitheism.

This, then, means that though atheism and antitheism are often blood brothers, atheism can be *more* than antitheism. When, for example, it denies all gods, it confronts believers who may not be theists as well as those who are theists.

At this point we may not find this distinction between atheism and antitheism very important, but when it comes time to make judgments about con-

[4] *Modern Atheism* (London: Burns & Oates, 1961), p. 8.

temporary atheism, the excursion should be of help to us.

THE UNIQUENESS OF CONTEMPORARY ATHEISM

Our study of atheism is further complicated by the fact that much of contemporary atheism appears different from classical atheism. Why is this so?

In the first place, much of classical atheism was bent on proving the nonexistence of God. Scholars and philosophers wrote mountains of books dedicated to the single task of proving in an intellectual fashion that there is no God. And as we shall see in a later chapter dealing with the church's answers to atheism, theologians and ecclesiastical leaders defended the theist's position with intellectual arguments. It is accurate to say that the adherents of classical atheism spent much time in intellectual gymnastics, trying to convince others through logic and argumentation that God does not exist.

But the most powerful kind of contemporary atheism does not spend a great deal of time debating the issue of God's existence or nonexistence. Whole systems of modern atheism simply *start with the assumption that there is no God.* Put another way, whereas classical atheism was preoccupied with the blocks of knowledge and the pyramids of logical arguments which disproved the existence of God, contemporary atheism *begins* its witness with the conviction that there is no God and that we had best get on with things.

This beginning is often disarming and even devastating to the theist eager to confront atheism. But it is nevertheless a typical characteristic of much contemporary atheism, especially Marxist atheism, which will draw our attention in a later chapter.

A second characteristic of contemporary atheism, unlike classical atheism, is its growing and obvious *popularity among ordinary people*. Historically, the atheistic position has been proposed by a very small minority of the world's population. For the most part these adherents have been intellectual revolutionaries and have represented only a splinter group amid the great clod of humanity.

For example, not many of the world's truly great thinkers have been atheists. Yet there has been a small but very articulate group of such men. In the late nineteenth century Friedrich Nietzsche, the German philosopher, wrote, "God is dead"; and his thesis, along with some of his other teachings, caused many ripples and waves in the world not the smallest of which was Hitler's national socialism. Later Marx and Engels, the founders of modern communism, built their idea of dialectic materialism on an atheistic tradition started in France in the mid-nineteenth century, thus initiating a movement which has by now touched the lives of just about every person in the world. In America the educational philosopher John Dewey taught a form of atheism in that his system left no room for the supernatural; today his naturalistic pragmatism fingers its way throughout America's public school system. And, of course, the great psychologist Sigmund Freud brought an atheistic assumption into his understanding of human nature.

Seen in the larger context of the world's great thinkers, this is not a very impressive group numberwise, despite the obviously significant impact of their teaching on the modern world. Even admitting that such a listing is fragmentary and arbitrary, we still cannot help but be struck by the fact that the atheistic stance has been taken by a relatively small fellowship of scholars. And what is perhaps more important, their teachings were known by only a fraction of the world's population.

Today atheism is something quite different. Though it is still true that in America only about one percent of the population claims atheism as its position, the percentage of unbelievers in Europe is considerable. Anyone who has spent time in Europe knows that more and more people there are seemingly quite able to round out their lives without making any significant reference to God or to their Christian tradition.

Perhaps the following words by a psychoanalyst and priest, formerly a confirmed atheist, depict the point in ample fashion:

Contemporary atheism, at least in the developed countries of Christian civilization, is distinguished from the

atheism of other times and other civilizations above all by
its extension. It is no longer a phenomenon of a few individuals protesting against the taboos of society, nor the
privilege of a minority who consider themselves especially
"enlightened" in the manner of the eighteenth century
rationalists. It is the common lot of at least a considerable
portion, if not of the majority, of our contemporaries and
is well on its way to becoming the common norm of society. The intellectuals were the first to break with traditional faith; the bourgeois followed them; then came the
masses, and, finally, the peasants.[5]

Besides the widespread acceptance of atheism in
the world and the tendency of modern atheism to
start from the assumption that there is no God, there
is a third characteristic of contemporary atheism
which sets it apart significantly from classical atheism:
*the tendency to base the atheistic position on a high
concept of morality and a sensitivity to man's finite
condition.*

Frequently in the past the atheist has been a dogmatic, argumentative, arrogant fellow not usually concerned with matters of ethics and morality. It was
not unusual for classical atheism to criticize the whole
area of ethical responsibility.

These characteristics are not found in much contemporary atheism, which sees man as a finite being
who must live and work out his destiny in a world

[5] Ignace Lepp, *Atheism in Our Time* (New York: The Macmillan Co., 1963), p. 6.

which he did not create. He and all other men caught up in the web of reality, forced into a position where everyone needs everyone else. Men are truly brothers—not because they are the children of a loving God, but because they are alone in a world of unbearable sorrow and suffering. To be an atheist is to recognize this awful fact and still to work out one's destiny within it, not expecting any help from heaven or a book of wisdom.

In this situation men must come to value one another and to see themselves as true brothers, such brotherhood being defined by the facts of life. Under these circumstances men are not "good" in order to please an angry God, but because goodness is the only sane condition of men who share so completely the awesome terror of the catastrophic threat which continuously hangs over mankind.

ATHEISM AND ITS MODIFIERS

By this time the reader might wish to return to one of the literal meanings of atheism. "Belief that there is no God" may seem a pleasant and soothing definition amid the confusion I have surely by this time created. But accepting such a position will not help us understand atheism, and surely to misunderstand it or oversimplify it would not contribute to the search set for us by our Christian faith.

The fact is, of course, there can be no one definition of atheism. Nor is it possible to arrive at a definition which would be acceptable to all. If, indeed, we insist on holding to a single definition, we are bound to stretch it to such a point that it becomes quite meaningless—all to satisfy the demands honestly placed upon us by the outer turmoil of the world and by the inner spirit of our faith. On the other hand, if we settle for a very narrow definition of atheism, we surely will find, if we are honest, that we must mistreat badly many searching souls who call themselves atheists but simply cannot be placed in a narrow category. What, then, is left for us to do?

I should like to suggest that we examine atheism with the help of modifiers rather than from the point of view of a single meaning. A modifier alters the basic form. It may do this by adding or subtracting or simply changing in some way the original meaning. Such a practice still permits us to hold to the basic or literal definition, at the same time permitting us flexibility enough to appreciate the richness of the contemporary meanings frequently attached to the word "atheism."

Of course, there is an arbitrary factor to be recognized for after all, modifiers might be many. For example, writers have used the following, among others: scientific atheism, Christian atheism, practical atheism, unconscious atheism, Marxist atheism, and so forth. But the purpose of our study can lift us out of this dilemma. We are primarily interested in learning about the forms of *contemporary* atheism and especially those types or kinds of contemporary atheism which seem to have a very special relevance for the Christian layman. In making this effort, therefore, I should like to concentrate on the following three modifiers: Marxist, Christian, and unconscious. This is not to withdraw attention from other modifiers, only to concentrate on these three options.

Actually, modifiers such as these must be seen in relation to the basic or literal meaning of atheism; that is, in studying Marxist, Christian, and unconscious atheism we cannot lose sight of the literal meaning. Indeed, the peculiar relations of these modifiers to the literal meaning will often represent the meat of our understanding.

But before turning to these three modified forms of atheism we will need to gain some insight into the way atheism, no matter what its form, comes about. Chapter two will deal with this problem.

SUMMARY

Atheism is not a simple, one-dimensional word. Although its literal meaning states the negative assertion that there is no God, both historic and contemporary atheism have attempted to communicate a broader meaning than this. In the past, atheists were frequently misunderstood or dismissed without a hearing. Their minority helped account for this. Also, atheism itself was seen, especially by Christians, as an immoral stance. Other factors which cloud any comprehensive understanding of atheism are: (1)

the confusion over the differences between literal atheism—the assertion that there is no God—and agnosticism—the doctrine that we cannot know whether there is a God or not; (2) the failure to see clearly and appreciate fully the differences and affinities between atheism and antitheism; (3) the tendency to think of atheism in its literal sense only, thus ignoring the great differences between much of classical atheism and much of contemporary atheism, especially that form of contemporary atheism which *starts* from the basic atheistic position rather than ending with it.

Because of the complexity and rich meaning found in contemporary atheism, it is not possible to obtain a Christian understanding of atheism by treating it as a single, narrow, one-dimensional system of thought. Though the literal meaning of atheism needs to serve as a basis for our study, various modifiers must be used to do justice to contemporary atheism. Marxist atheism, Christian atheism, and unconscious atheism are types which appear characteristic of a great deal of contemporary atheism and which have a very special relationship to the practicing Christian.

2. How Atheism Comes About

An illusion shared by everyone becomes a reality.
—Erich Fromm

Man positively needs general ideas and convictions that will give a meaning to his life and enable him to find a place for himself in the universe.
—Carl Gustav Jung

Within the past several decades scholars have spent a great deal of time and effort in trying to discover the roots of the religious life. Historians, anthropologists, sociologists, and psychologists have been especially interested in finding a single motive which might explain how religion began. Though all of these efforts have produced interesting theories as to the origin of the religious sentiment, not one appears adequate to embrace the apparent complexity of religious beliefs. In fact, most reputable scholars now agree that there is probably no one single cause giving rise to religious behavior. Rather, it is probably safer to assume that religion begins, both in the primitive and the modern citizen, as a result of many forces.

We might assume, I think, that atheism too cannot be explained in any simple way. We might wish to suppose that the answer to the question, "How does atheism come about?" would be a simple one. A psychologist, for example, might like to believe that a person becomes an atheist because he was unable to develop a sense of trust in his formative years. Or an historian might wish to explain the rise of religion in terms of the development of agriculture in the Mesopotamian valley, claiming that the lack of technical information had to be replaced with superstitions of rain gods and storm gods. Now that technology has developed, the need for gods disappears leaving a citizenry of atheists. Or the anthropologists might claim that religion originated to eliminate the presence of "cognitive discomfort," which came about because man, especially primitive man, could not understand himself or the world in which he lived.

Our attempt to understand atheism will not be quite as ambitious as these global theories. We are not especially interested in speculating about the possibility of a single beginning of the atheistic stance. The fact is that atheism like all beliefs probably has many roots, and some of them may not be nearly as deep or complicated as scholars would lead us to think.

For instance, when Euripides, the fifth-century-B.C. poet, was accused of being an atheist, a woman

38

expressed this kind of reasoning to help verify the poet's guilt:

> Ladies, I've only a few words to add.
> I quite agree with the honourable lady
> Who has just sat down: she has spoken well and ably.
> But I can tell you what I've borne myself.
> My husband died in Cyprus, leaving me
> Five little chicks to work and labour for.
> I've done my best, and bad's the best, but still
> I've fed them, weaving chaplets for the Gods.
> But now this fellow writes his plays, and says
> There are no Gods; and so, you might depend,
> My trade is fallen to half; men won't buy chaplets.
> So then for many reasons he must die;
> The man is bitterer than his mother's potherbs.
> I leave my cause with you, my sisters: I
> Am called away on urgent private business,
> An order, just received, for twenty chaplets.[1]

No great metaphysical argument here! We get the impression that this woman's beliefs have some pretty simple and practical roots. We can feel some empathy for the poor poet who probably arrived at his atheistic position by a process far less utilitarian than that by which the lady arrived at her religious belief!

The fact is, of course, that atheism like theism may

---

[1] Aristophanes, *The Thesmophoriazusae*, Benjamin Bickley Rodgers, trans., in Vol. 5 of "Great Books of the Western World" (Chicago: Encyclopaedia Britannica, 1952), p. 605.

have many roots and many explanations. Our purpose in this chapter is not to identify all the possible motives for becoming an atheist. Rather we want to take a look at a sample of reasons why people come to the position of contemporary atheism. The hope is that such a sampling will help us to understand the principle of multiple causation as well as to secure an appreciation of the complexity of any attempt to explain atheism. Our topics will include the psychological roots of atheism, the reality of suffering, the impact of modern science, and the manifest failure of the Christian church.

PSYCHOLOGICAL ROOTS OF ATHEISM

Within the past fifty years psychologists have had a great deal to say about religious beliefs and attitudes. Psychoanalysis especially has come to some penetrating conclusions about why men believe in God. This great psychological system has claimed that religion is merely the projection of inner emotions, fears, and longings onto a cosmic plane; that is, our personal emotions are projected out into the universe. Belief in God, in other words, is a belief based on our associations with an earthly father.[2]

There are many similar theories and explanations, but strangely enough there are very few psychological

[2] For a brief summary of psychoanalysis' theory of religion see my *Mature Religion: A Psychological Study* (Nashville: Abingdon Press, 1965), especially chapter one.

explanations of unbelief. Yet, we would suppose, if belief can be explained in psychological terms, so too can atheism.

Psychologists have identified at least four psychological motives which help explain the atheistic position. First, atheism may be the result of a *revolt against authority*. Many a young man desperately desires to overthrow his father. In the process he might also cast down the God of his father. Often revolt against father is generalized to all authority, including the traditional authority of the church and of God. Personal and specific revolt is transformed into general revolt, and atheism is born in the midst of this emotional complex.

Second, atheism may have its roots in a man's deep *yearning for power*. Alfred Adler, the great psychologist and founder of individual psychology, once wrote, "I began to see clearly in every psychological phenomenon the striving for superiority. It runs parallel to physical growth and is an intrinsic necessity of life itself. It lies at the root of all solutions of life's problems and is manifested in the way in which we meet these problems. All our functions follow its direction. They strive for conquest, security, increase, either in the right or in the wrong direction. The impetus from minus to plus never ends. The urge from below to above never ceases. Whatever premises all our philosophers and psychologists dream of— self-preservation, pleasure principle, equalization—

all these are but vague representations, attempts to express the great upward drive." [3]

If a man is driven by such a need for power and superiority, it would seem that the idea of an all-powerful God would be distasteful. Friedrich Nietzsche once confessed, "If there were gods, how could I endure it to be no god?" Such an extreme statement illustrates how an emotional need for superiority can lead one to deny the gods.

Third, atheism may be the result of *projection*, the tendency to avoid blame by placing the responsibilities upon others. Since God made me, *he* is responsible for my misdeeds. Or, if God and the belief in immortality are cast out of my thoughts, then there is nothing to fear in either this world or the next, and thus I am freed from any sense of "ought" or obligation.

Fourth, atheism may be the end result of the conquest of desire over reason, of what the psychologists call *rationalization*. Inner and outer forces may drive an individual to formulate all kinds of explanations in order to overcome psychological discomfort. A person who feels alone and isolated in a world against which he must defend himself may conclude that there is no God. An individual overwhelmed by economic and social responsibilities, feeling that he and

[3] Alfred Adler, *The Individual Psychology of Alfred Adler*, Heinz L. Ansbacher and Rowena R. Ansbacher, eds. (New York: Basic Books, 1956), p. 103.

he alone suffers under such a heavy burden, may conclude that he is indeed alone.

There are many inner weaknesses, psychological cripplings, which a person does not wish to accept in himself. Under such circumstances it is not unlikely that the individual will try to find cosmic reasons to explain his own inadequacies.

Are there other psychological roots which might help explain the development of atheistic attitudes? According to some psychologists and psychiatrists, there is in man a general need to find meaning in life. Such a propensity might be considered a kind of blanket psychological need which could give rise to any number of explanations, including the one called atheism. Sometimes, as psychoanalysts often point out, certain experiences in life drive people to theism, to a belief in a God removed from the world yet active in it. In this fashion, argue these psychologists, the awful conditions of the world become more tolerable because there is a personal God who under proper conditions can do something about it—if not now, later on. Such a projection gives meaning to life.

What is not usually recognized by these psychologists is that these very same conditions also can lead to disbelief. The individual may be overcome by pressures of life. He may, especially after failing to find relief in a theistic formulation, sit down in the midst of his turmoil and conclude that there is no power or force beyond. There is only a void. This conclusion injects *meaning* into his condition. He now knows why things are so bad—there is nothing out there controlling or helping him—and he can now get on with life on another level. Thus the same psychological condition leading to a commitment to a theistic position can lead to an atheistic one.

We must spend a bit more time on the nature of the psychological explanation for atheism because frequently more "noble" explanations are but disguises of this one. Perhaps if we see the psychological process at work in a particular individual, we will have a better understanding of how this dynamic works. A former Marxist, now a Catholic psychotherapist, gives us this account of a young girl's flight to atheism:

Lisa confided to the psychiatrists who examined her that she gave up her faith because, thanks to existentialist philosophy, she understood that "it was all nonsense." She discovered that life was "rotten," absolutely absurd. She saw no reason to restrain herself from a pleasure or a caprice for which she felt a slight attraction. Neither her own dignity nor that of her parents seemed worthy of interest. Family, country, Church—all of this was part of the enterprise of mystification. She proudly quoted Kafka, Camus' *The Stranger*, and especially Jean-Paul Sartre. . . .

Gradually, Lisa revealed that it was not primarily intellectual evidence that turned her from a pious schoolgirl into an atheist existentialist. About a year before her crisis, she had spent her vacation with a classmate who belonged to a high select Catholic environment. There she met a man whose fame was already well established. This distinguished person took an interest in Lisa, directed her reading, and encouraged her idealistic and enthusiastic penchants. Lisa was so enthralled with the friendship that she offered no resistance whatsoever when the man asked her to become his mistress. Unfortunately, after several months of passionate happiness, the man grew tired of her charms and abandoned her in the name of the work he had to accomplish, and with which Lisa's love presumably interfered. Lisa became totally disillusioned and what followed was but the logical consequences of her deception. How could there be anything great or sacred in the world, if even a man of this distinction was really no more than a cad? She had naturally heard of Sartre and other masters of "the existentialism of despair." She read them with the desire of finding a philosophical confirmation and justification of her personal experience. Then came the blue jeans, the existentialist cellars, the petty crimes, and her involvement in a murder. She was quite convinced that existentialist philosophy was the basis of her revolt. She believed that she acted absurdly, because life itself was absurd and that she should not be conspicuous by her good behavior.[4]

Here we see how personal emotional experiences may lead, through a complex process of rationalization, to the atheistic position. Though the roots of atheism were deeply entwined in emotional conflicts, Lisa refused to consider these deep and dynamic factors. Rather, far more noble and intellectual factors

[4] Lepp, *Atheism in Our Time*, pp. 157-58.

are drawn upon to explain her position of unbelief.

Later, in the chapter dealing with unconscious atheism, we will look a bit more closely at this psychological explanation, but here I do feel compelled to note the danger of this kind of understanding. There is no doubt that psychological conflicts frequently are at the source of the belief systems put forth by men, including the atheists' arguments. But we must be very careful in concluding that all of atheism can be understood on purely psychological grounds. Such a tendency has been labeled *psychologism*, the doctrine which claims that psychology is the basis of all the sciences and that logic, ethics, and aesthetics rest on the facts of experience alone.

Though we must never forget the great and abiding power of the psychological explanation of atheism and though we ought to keep in mind that psychological reactions are always present and influential in the development of unbelief, there are other aspects of reality which need to be identified if we are to appreciate the mosaic rootage of contemporary atheism.

THE REALITY OF SUFFERING

Though it would be difficult to prove in any conclusive way, it would appear that one of the major reasons driving men of faith into the stockade of atheism is the stark fact of human suffering and evil. I say "fact" because I believe that no sane and thoughtful person can consistently deny the awful and obvious reality of suffering and affliction in the world today.

There is no need here to turn to ancient or modern authorities, no need to quote from the mountains of volumes written both to acknowledge and to "explain" suffering and evil. All we need to do is to look about, scan the evening paper, glimpse within the circle of our personal life and experiences. One devout Christian looked back on his life and felt compelled to write, "Unable to sleep I have asked myself whether there is a God who is interested in the fate of the individual. I find it hard to believe so, for this God has permitted a few hundred thousand men bestialized, insane or blinded to drown mankind in rivers of blood and agony and crush it under mountains of horror and despair. He lets millions of decent people suffer and die without raising a finger. Is this justice? Is not this sort of collective punishment the reverse of justice?" [5]

And it does not take a worldwide epidemic of nazism to make us think such thoughts. Recall, for example, that day when an American atomic bomb fell on the Japanese city of Hiroshima. No matter how we may rationalize such an act, the stark fact remains that innocent children fried to death at their mothers' breasts. This is the awful and inexplicable fact. No

[5] Gerhard Ritter, *The German Resistance*, R. T. Clark, trans. (New York: Frederick A. Praeger, 1958), pp. 309-10.

47

word beyond this can be said which will change that fact.

Of course, as Christians we have heard all the arguments set forth to explain why it is that suffering and evil sear the earth while a good and compassionate God watches over us. We have heard that pain is good in itself or that it has no real existence. We have heard the claim that pain and suffering are the natural results of prior sin, that God too is limited and suffers with us, that suffering is itself a disguised form of good, and so forth. We have been told, and some of us have been convinced, that it was man who grabbed the fruit of knowledge, and now he is only reaping what comes to those who disobey God's directives. Some of these arguments are noble and grand. Fortunately for many, these theories and theologies apparently suffice or at least make the situation a tolerable one for millions of people.

A few seem ready to accept the theologians' argument which tells us that we simply do not understand God and therefore we do not understand the necessity of evil and suffering. Other Christians seem to see that it is indeed foolish to look for God in such a horrid mixture of good and evil; surely goodness must originate *outside* of this world!

But some are unable to lift a faith out of the pit. For thousands of sincere and sensitive souls no rational explanation is nearly strong enough to overcome the constant scraping and tearing of human flesh. To these people—and there are literally millions of them—a good God and a suffering world simply do not make sense. In the face of the empirical evidence which engulfs them, they must conclude that there is no God.

THE IMPACT OF MODERN SCIENCE

If certain men are plagued by the reality of evil and suffering, a far larger number are awed by the accomplishments of modern science. Sigmund Freud ended his analysis and criticism of the Christian faith with these words of commitment to science: "No, our science is no illusion. But an illusion it would be to suppose that what science cannot give us we can get elsewhere." [6] And this essentially is the spirit of modern science although most of us might not articulate our faith in it with the straightforward clarity shown by Freud.

But the fact remains that modern science is esteemed by the majority of mankind and that most members of an affluent society believe in science to a staggering degree. Though few of us may know a great deal about the inner workings of the scientific world, all of us can easily see and appreciate the fabulous advances in technology which are the result of the scientific method and spirit.

Indeed, the Christian community now spends a great deal of its time trying to demonstrate that there

[6] Sigmund Freud, *The Future of an Illusion* (rev. Anchor Book ed.; New York: Doubleday & Co., 1964), p. 92.

is no real conflict between science and religion, despite the fact that history and common sense point up quite a different kind of relationship. Some noble and penetrating attempts to show that religion and science are complementary and mutually helpful communities have been advanced; nevertheless, there are millions of men who see them as mutually exclusive approaches. In fact, there is a significant segment of the world's population (as will be noted in the chapter dealing with Marxist atheism) which holds that it is science which confronts humanity with the questions of its being and destiny, not philosophy or religion, which traditionally have done so.

Just a brief excursion into the history and nature of science will give some indication of how the contemporary view of science was born. Several hundred years before Christ the Epicureans taught that science must accept two fundamental principles. First, it should take account of all the evidence available, and second, it should not explain perplexing phenomena by referring to the possible intervention of the gods. In a very real sense this Greek philosophy of science was the beginning of what might be called methodological atheism.

Indeed, it can be argued that all science by its very nature must be atheistic. That is, the scientist must exclude God from his work; he dare not use him to explain the workings of the universe. It is no accident that many great scientists—e.g., Descartes, Newton, Malebranche, and Gassendi—have been accused of being atheists. Certainly church history demonstrates dramatically that great scientists frequently got into trouble with church authorities, even to the point of being openly persecuted. Part of this tendency came about because scientific systems do not permit room for God as an explanatory factor. That this propensity has had tremendous effects on the development of contemporary atheism cannot be denied.

These assumptions do not only apply to the physical sciences. The great contemporary wave of social science exploration carries with it a similar claim and demand. Every attempt is being made to understand, predict, and control the behavior of man via the use of social science research and programs. Social science laws are being formulated with precision. Some scholars have even argued that once social science realizes its full potential, God will disappear from the minds and hearts of men.

Both the physical sciences and the social sciences are painting a new picture of man and the nature of his destiny. Science has driven out the sun-god, the sky-god, shamans, witch doctors, and primitive superstitions. Some sophisticated Christians would argue that such scientific accomplishments have purified our concept of God, but what science discovers we do not usually call God, nor do we see such discoveries as revelations of a good and omnipotent God. With the increasing control of science the differences between a religious and secular interpretation of the universe become insignificant, to say the least. Salvation through scientific knowledge is a solid and widespread factor, not only in the Communist countries, but in capitalist America and in western Europe. The belief that modern science is the new Messiah is a universal belief, demonstrated in the practical affairs of men everywhere. And, of course, there can be no room for two messiahs. Science, then, can and frequently does give rise to atheism.

THE FAILURE OF THE CHURCH

Another important factor contributing to the acceptance of modern atheism is the manifest failure of the Christian church in our time. Institutional religion is everywhere on the defensive. Critics are found in every sphere of human activity. Secularists and religionists alike wail over the obvious failure of the church. During the Nazi holocaust the German church—or at least most of it—cowed down before the authority of force and fanaticism, offering only weak resistance. The American church, facing the great wave of civil rights demands, did not assume a major leadership role, and even today the military establishment and the athletic community are far ahead of the church in the area of functional integration. Equally obvious is the fact that the church has joined culture, has taken on materialistic and opportunistic values of the "Great Society." In far too many instances it is difficult to distinguish between the church and the society before which it is called to witness.

This is certainly not to minimize or deny the good which has been done and is being done by organized religion. The object here is merely to point out that millions of people look at the church and see just another institution of culture, apparently organized to support a particular power structure. In the New Testament the good news was not regarded as subservient to any nation or political system. It did not exist to support civilization. But in its development and expansion it has come to be equated with such things as American democracy or capitalist economy or Western civilization. The critics see this shift clearly and precisely.

Of course, there are many good and reasonable arguments to explain why the church manages to adjust, to rationalize, to bend; but the point I wish to make here is that for many these maneuvers are signs that the church does not have any special or divine undergirding.

Equally important is the claim that committed Christians who have become disillusioned with their church rarely become converts to another world religion. Invariably the disillusioned Christian becomes an atheist of one type or another. There appears to be a strange dynamic involved in the disrupted beliefs, summarized perhaps perfectly, if briefly, by the words from a Catholic priest who left his church: "I now clearly see that it is impossible for a man who has lived the Christian faith intensely to believe in the God of the Bible outside the Church. And since I no longer believe in the Christian God, how could I possibly believe in other gods?" [7]

Thus it is that many turn to one or all the three forms of atheism to be reviewed in the next section of this book.

SUMMARY

The roots of atheism are many and complex. The Christian would err greatly if he settled for an oversimplified explanation. The psychological explanation—that atheism is the intellectual statement and result of deep and complex emotional problems—is undoubtedly true to a great degree. That various psychological mechanisms may lead to the atheistic stance cannot be denied. But the argument that atheism finds its sole explanation in the psychological realm is a form of psychologism which simply does not do justice to the complexity of life and the universe. Other aspects of reality which help form the atheistic mood must be acknowledged. One of these is the sheer fact of human sufferings and evils, which have driven thousands of sincere souls into the camp of atheism. Another aspect of reality is the nature of contemporary science, which has given millions the impression that God is not needed and that man

[7] Quoted in Lepp, *Atheism in Our Time*, p. 8.

can stand alone. Another fact of reality is that many people look upon the church as a failure, a sham in the light of its lofty claims, and therefore flee out of it and into one or all of the various atheistic positions especially prevalent in our day.

PART II

Kinds of Atheism

3. Marxist Atheism

All contemporary religions and churches, all and every kind of religious organization, Marxism has always viewed as organs of bourgeois reaction, serving as a defense of exploitation and the doping of the working-classes.

—Nikolai Lenin

The religious world is but the reflex of the real world.

—Karl Marx

In recent years the atheism of communism has attracted considerable attention from Christian theologians. Though there has never been any doubt about the fact that Karl Marx, the founder of modern communism, was an atheist, there has been some question about the functional ways the Communists have tried to carry out the program of world conquest and the spread of Marxist atheism. There have been times, for example, when Communist countries seemingly have taken a rather kind attitude toward organized religion. At other times their theoretical position has been acted out in clear and obvious persecution.

The Christian layman should not be confused over what appear to be conciliatory attitudes toward religion on the part of official communism. As we shall note in this chapter, the Communists have often shifted methods in dealing with religion, but there has never been a time in the development of the Communistic purpose when the ultimate elimination of Christianity was abandoned. Even in the "liberal" United Soviet Socialist Republic of today, the elimination of religion remains an assumed objective.

The major purpose of this chapter will not be to argue that modern Marxist communism has changed its basic conviction about religion; rather it will be to describe the extent of contemporary Marxist atheism, to examine its basic nature, to decide why communism must reject all religions, to appreciate the difficulties of reconciling communism and Christianity, to see how modern Marxists view Christianity, and to identify areas where Marxist atheism and Christianity seem to agree.

THE EXTENT OF MARXIST ATHEISM

If there is one outstanding fact about the world we live in, it is that atheism has become a political force of such power that its shadow is cast over one third of the world's population. With the rise of communism a third of mankind—nearly a thousand million souls—felt the weight of a form of materialism which influenced all earthly powers. The state was identi-

fied with an atheist church which regulated man's
conscience and even his private behavior. The leaders
of this new order are motivated by a conviction that
excludes all arguments from without. Atheism is a
prerequisite, not a debatable point. "This powerful
position occupied by atheism," writes Etienne Borne,
"raises some anxious questions. A force is powerful
less because of what it has done than because of what
it can still do. Communism is an all-embracing creed
which, like Islam in earlier centuries, joins in a single
will to expand spiritual and temporal ambition. Its
leaders believe in the infallibility of the Book received
from Marx and Lenin; and for its prophecies to be
accomplished it is necessary that all men shall one
day be Communists." [1]

This, it would appear, is the true extent and
nature of modern communism. If the picture is
accurate, it is not a pleasant picture—not at any rate
from a Christian perspective. It is frightening, to say
the least. And though we Christians, always in search
of hope and positive interpretations, may desire *not*
to see modern communism in such powerful terms,
we had best start by facing the reality of our enemy.
Modern Marxist atheism, as an integral part of world
communism, is a mass phenomenon, and its stern
intolerance intends to rule over the *whole* future of
mankind.

This means that we are not asked to deal with a

[1] *Modern Atheism*, p. 85.

splinter of thought in opposition to the general Christian world view. Instead we are confronted with a force whose magnitude is of tidal wave proportion, a force whose dominant aim is to cast its shadow across the entire world and to allow not a single flicker of light from any other competing force or system of thought.

What, then, is the nature of this tremendously ambitious conviction called Marxist atheism?

THE NATURE OF MARXIST ATHEISM

In an attempt to point up the basic nature of Marxist atheism, I shall offer five characteristics with brief explanation, all in the hope that such a summary will serve as a stimulus for discussion and reflection rather than as an exhaustive catalog of Marxist atheism.

First, Marxist atheism is decidedly *dogmatic in theory and in practice*. Of course, any form of totalitarian system must be intolerant of doubt or skepticism directed against it. Marxism generally, and specifically when it comes to atheism, is a doctrine of truth in which total commitment is required. There is absolutely no room for any uncertainty of thought, not even for hesitation.

In the case of the atheistic stance this dogmatic requirement means that it is impossible to be an agnostic Marxist, for an agnostic does not know whether there is a God or not. But the loyal Marxist *does* know: *there is no God!*

At first such dogmatism may appear strange to the Christian who has a kind of tentative faith; that is, though he may be certain to the point of pouring his life into his faith, he is not cocksure to the point of excluding the possibility of any other claim. But the Christian must remember always that Marxism seen within is not simply another world view, one among many; rather, it is a revolutionary creed. Good Marxist doctrine claims that man's knowledge of himself eliminates completely even the possibility that there might be a God. Man's essential and ultimate being is in *work*, which he uses to adapt nature to himself. Man through work creates his own conditions for existence and, in fact, creates himself. In such a closed system the very inkling that there might be a Being beyond the system is an intolerable intrusion.

Second, Marxist atheism sees its assertions as being *built exclusively on modern science.* To the Marxist, atheism is the logical and most reasonable position to hold if one is aware of the methods and findings of contemporary science. Any other conclusion is at best a mistake.

This aspect of Marxist atheism has a real pull in the contemporary world. As one scholar notes: "Marxist atheism embodies an important aspect of modern life. Scientific thought, research, discovery, technical progress—all this means so much for present-day modern man that he will not take seriously any approach to reality which does not measure up to this precision of thought. For a generation which believes in the encyclopedia, in statistics, in experimentation, and in other forms of expression of scientific thought, precision of thought and terminology is an indispensable presupposition. In contrast to the widespread tendency within Christendom to substitute emotional generalities for clear convictions of faith, Marxist religious thought will always prove superior." [2]

But Marxist atheism has appeal on other grounds than the popularity of modern science. The most precision-minded man, the most reasonable and educated person, the most ardent of scholars, might find this phase of communism especially appealing. For Marxism claims that nature—that which we can see, touch, manipulate—contains in itself all the laws of its own development. This autodynamism, as the Communist textbooks call it, is the key to the entire understanding of mankind. Every conceivable event can find meaning within nature and history, thus eliminating once and for all the illusions of the supernatural or the transhistoric. All historic forces lead to a humanity which is, thanks to the death of God, its own providence and its own reason to be. Thus science is not so much the basis of atheism as it is rather its inevitable cohort in progress.

[2] Hanns Lilje, *Atheism, Humanism, and Christianity* (Minneapolis, Minn.: Augsburg Publishing House, 1964), p. 17.

Third, Marxist atheism is *invariably and especially antichristian.* Since its beginning, Marxist atheism has had a special hatred for Christianity. Though its atheistic thesis excludes *all* religions from its purview, it has directed much of its criticism not against religion in general, but against the Christian religion. We might well ask, "Why is this so?"

One major reason may be found in Marxism's concept of history. Historical materialism teaches that there are "moments" in history when certain forces play an important part in the unfolding of the communist intention, even though such forces have no affinity with the socialistic plan itself. These forces, or systems, merely play a part in the dialectical evolution of mankind. Christianity represents such a moment.

Christianity's claim that its central message is absolute truth, applicable to all times and all conditions, played an important part in the development of the communistic thesis. For such a claim, once the conditions of mankind changed, naturally led to a reactionary and conservative stance. And this inevitable inclination provided a necessary step in the evolutionary process. In this sense Christianity has rendered considerable service to the Communist cause.

But, note the Communists, it has now played out its part and is no longer needed. This is one reason why, as we shall note in detail later, communism frequently ignores the Christian church; even to recognize it via persecution would indicate that the natural decay has not really taken place as predicted.

Christianity both as a faith and as an institution appears to pop up unexpectedly and with irritating claims. Such occurrences are embarrassing to basic Marxist doctrine and partially explain why Marxist atheism is especially directed toward Christian theism.

Without falling into the trap of psychologism we must note that Marx himself manifested a peculiar hatred for Christianity. Contemporary psychiatrists have noted, for instance, that Marx showed a personal hatred for Christianity similar to that manifested by Freud, who, also a Jew, lived in a world that pretended to be Christian, one in which he himself could not find a home. Both Marx and Freud frequently bumped their heads against the "Christian" culture of the Europe of their time. Resentment, both conscious and unconscious, was the inevitable result. Such an emotional element, coupled with the "historic explanation" of the role of Christianity, goes a long way in helping us to see why Marxist atheism is especially antichristian in its orientation.

Fourth, Marxist atheism is *convinced that man must be the supreme being for man.* Perhaps if it were possible to identify a single basic belief of Marxist atheism which would separate it clearly from Christian theism, it would be Marx's doctrine of man. For Marx, religion originates from man's impotence in the presence of blind forces. This tendency alienates man from his fellowmen because in his

66

desperate desire to "do something" the good he does do he projects outward and believes that God is such goodness. This dynamic is true of religion, the family, the state, and so forth; and *all* these institutions prevent man from seeing that it is he and he alone who does and is these values. When man returns to a truly social mode of existence, he will come to see that it is neither necessary nor accurate to see the best of the world in anything or anyone beyond man himself.

This doctrine directly concerns itself with the conviction that modern man must break free from all those claims that are an obstacle to his liberty and his dignity. For Marxist atheism, Christianity has bound men to superstition, to economic determinism, and to fear. Man must now stand upright and claim his *human* dignity not because he is the son of God, but simply because he is *man*.

Fifth, Marxist atheism is *existential in practice.* By this I mean that modern Marxist atheism is not simply an intellectual doctrine which can be accepted tongue in cheek. Our discussion of the basically dogmatic character of this assumption points in this direction. The typical Marxist does not simply and passively accept atheism as one doctrine among many. Rather he sees it as an absolute necessity and one which is an integral part of the entire Communist structure. Though pragmatic Marxists may at times appear tolerant of religion, this can only be a delayed kind of attitude, for the true Marxist must believe

67

with his whole being that if his approach to life is right then religion's approaches must be wrong. The point here is that this conviction is *complete* and *comprehensive*. It is not a splinter policy which can be considered unimportant or casual.

We shall now see why Marxist atheism must be existential, must be exclusive and overwhelming in its demands.

The Exclusive Nature of Communism

A modern man of thought and faith would not find it difficult to understand Marxist atheism. After all, it is a world view set on projecting meaning into life. In this sense it is no different from other attempts to organize what we find in the world. Yet there are an insistence and a demand in communism which place a requirement on its adherents quite beyond that demanded in many other systems of belief.

In the Communist system there is absolutely no room for religion. Actually, this demand is not difficult to understand if we remember that from its very beginning world communism was out to create a new man and that this new man would come about through man's efforts alone. This is an important point. It is not that no other system has ever set out to create a new man. Indeed, Christianity openly asserts that men must be made new in Christ, but this transformation is set in motion through what is given to man by God. It is God's grace as revealed in the

68

life, death, and resurrection of Christ which makes the new man possible.

But for communism this creation is *man's*. According to the founder of modern communism, religion always introduces an external or transcendent factor. And as long as man believes that a better life is available beyond history, he will not put forth the necessary effort to create a new man. He will come to depend upon forces beyond life and history as he has in the past.

Atheism, then, becomes an exclusive and integral part of the Communist system. There can be no place for religion in the mind of the modern Communist. Perhaps this point can be emphasized further by realizing that religion often has been viewed as a private affair between an individual and his God. Schleiermacher once defined religion as "a feeling of absolute dependence upon God." And Alfred North Whitehead, the famous American philosopher, once said that religion "is what the individual does with his own solitariness." No matter what our feelings about the inadequacies of such ideas of religion, the elements of dependence and privateness are present in most religions, especially Christianity.

These two stresses make religion impossible in the Communist world view, and for two very pointed reasons. First, in a Communist society man must be public. He is to be a new being completely dedicated to a new ideology. Unlike more traditional atheists, Marxist atheists are not content simply to write off religion as an illusion. Since communism's aim is the radical transformation of the world and of man, it requires that the whole person must openly and publicly show his commitment. The very idea that there can be a private part of life which falls outside the control of the party is an intolerable possibility. A Communist party member must *be* that. There can be no reservation and certainly no possibility of an inner life since such a life implies that it might be in conflict with the aims of world communism. And since religion is quite often an inner dynamic, it becomes especially repugnant to a Communist world view.

Second, the religious thesis that we are dependent upon a Power or Truth beyond ourselves is an unbearable teaching from the Communist's point of view. The teachings of world communism are very clear on this score. Man, if he is to be transformed, must transform himself. The danger is that man will not be willing to make the necessary sacrifices for communism if he has the slightest hint that there might be an active Truth greater than, or even similar to, that truth preached by the state. For a Communist to entertain the possibility that there is a Power or Truth beyond man is to introduce an uncontrollable factor into his faith in Communist doctrine. This is a definite danger, possibly a crippling one; therefore, Marxist atheism must be the official stance for modern communism.

Christian laymen should be perfectly clear on these

two points, for they help to explain why it has been and remains impossible to reconcile basic Christianity with basic Marxist communism.

Of course, as we have seen in the recent strains between China and Russia, Communist doctrine can bend and adjust too. But the bedrock positions of communism and Christianity are grossly at odds. This is not to deny the possibility of coexistence, but it does make even this a hard kind of relationship. Nor should Christians conclude that Communist doctrine has yielded in recent years just because apparently it has demonstrated a growing tolerance toward the church and religion. The reasons for this obvious tolerance should be appreciated by Christian laymen and will now attract our attention.

COMMUNISM'S ATTITUDE TOWARD RELIGION

We might begin our understanding of modern communism's attitude toward religion by realizing that Marx himself, though completely atheistic, did not spend a great deal of time attacking Christianity. It was not even worth his mental efforts! Marx's original attitude toward religion was basically one of near apathy and unconcern, a kind of I-could-care-less mood. Marx was saying that Christianity is not even an enemy worth fighting since it is already fading and near death.

This uncomplimentary attitude toward religion, and especially toward Christianity, still represents the

main official policy of world communism. The fact
that some modern Communist countries have
openly persecuted the church is more a slipping of
basic policy than it is an official and conscious shifting
of policy. Though there have been differences in
emphases among Soviet leaders—between Lenin and
Marx, for example—there has never been any doubt
whatsoever as to the primary thesis: *it is impossible to
conceive of the possibility of the survival of religion
in the Communist state.*

As Christians, however, we frequently misinterpret
communism's attitudes toward religion when we observe what appear to be changes in policy toward
churches. We must keep in mind that world communism *assumes* that religion will disappear.
Religion does not need to be openly persecuted or
violently destroyed. The tactic, thoroughly a part of
the Communist plan, is picturesquely put forth in
these words by Jean Lacroix:

"Why attack the idea of God?" asks Nadeau. "It seems
quite capable of falling apart of its own accord. It is
dangerous only on the level of historical and social development. For development takes place under the influence of struggles far removed from those of reason and
belief. It seems to me of very little moment that employer
and employee, both Christians, meet in the same church.
It is not in church, but in the factory, that their real life
is found." Atheism is then sometimes no more than the
denial of a problem which, were it a real one, would be
the most pressing of all. But the problem of God can be

pronounced unreal and mythical, for it no longer divides man.[3]

What does all this mean to the contemporary Christian who does take his faith seriously? For one thing it means that Marxist atheism is a different kind of thought than most atheistic positions held in the past. Traditionally, much atheism has been militant toward religion. It has seen Christianity as a major force to be reckoned with, a force to be destroyed in vigorous persecution. For the Christian, the lion in the street was clearly the enemy and could be seen as such.

But Marxist atheism is a given thought pattern which, to the ardent Communist at any rate, is a natural and perfectly reasonable stance. It is part of a larger pattern. And that which contradicts it—especially Christianity—is simply a shadowy movement, hardly worth the time and energy to face as a bona fide enemy. The assumption is that religion, including Christianity, is simply one of man's bad mistakes, but one which will be corrected with the unfolding of history and the spread of Communist teachings.

MARXISM AS RELIGION

Often when Christians are confronted with this picture of modern communism, they fall back on

[3] Jean Lacroix, *The Meaning of Modern Atheism* (New York: The Macmillan Co., 1965), pp. 15-16.

the argument that there are basic religious needs in mankind which will resist atheistic positions. There are deep and abiding reasons why religions have survived for thousands of years and that any atheism, including Marxist atheism, cannot destroy these metaphysical longings.

Whether there are deep and abiding needs in men which require a belief in theism is a neat and tantalizing question. But the Christian would do well not to answer contemporary Marxist atheism with this argument alone. For the fact is that communism is itself able to provide experiences quite similar to those offered by traditional Christianity.

As already stated, communism does place a certain demand on the individual's private life, often part of the role played by the Christian faith. Indeed, the similarity between organized world communism and the old Roman Catholic Church is in many ways striking. The concept of the Kremlin parallels the Middle Age concept of the Vatican. The frequent Communist purges are quite similar to the holy Inquisitions, and the Kremlin's list of forbidden books is longer than the Vatican's. There are even reports that "baptisms" and marriages in Russia frequently take on definite religious characteristics.

The point is that Marxist atheism frequently plays the same psychological role as traditional Christian faith. The fact seems to be that contemporary Marxist atheism can fulfill many needs historically met by organized religion.

It may be rightly argued that this is not the same as saying that modern communism meets the basic *spiritual* needs of mankind. Yet the bland fact remains that millions of Russian and Chinese people are born, reared, and move through adulthood without the beliefs, practices, and values traditionally communicated by the church and by the Christian faith generally.

AGREEMENTS BETWEEN MARXISM AND CHRISTIANITY

The Christian desirous of peace and yearning for a better world of healthy relationships may see Marxist atheism as a wall far too high and too thick to be touched by his tappings. Yet every Christian must seriously wonder if there is any common ground whatsoever between world communism and the Christian faith. From the above discussion it would appear that any real relationship between a genuine Christian faith and an orthodox Marxism is impossible. The only answer seems to be in the belief that one of the systems will need to die or be converted. Certainly to many Christians and Marxists alike this appears to be the only solution to the obvious split presently existing in the world.

Yet there does appear to be one strangely comprehensive thesis to which we find men of goodwill dedicated in a potentially positive way. We might call this simply the desire that man be himself and that he seek to live on this earth in harmony and productivity with his fellowmen.

Lenin once said, "Religion is a kind of bad spiritual vodka in which the slaves of capitalism drown their human nature and the resentment which stems from a life that is so unworthy of man." Most intelligent men, whether Christian or not, must admit that these words *do* characterize a great deal of what has passed for religion in Western civilization. No one can honestly review the history of the civilized world, including church history itself, without seeing that religion often has degraded and dehumanized man. It has far too often fed superstition and supported power structures, and during certain periods it has played the role of a conceited ass, as far removed from its Lord's spirit as it could possibly get. While theologians wrangled over the question of how many angels could dance on the point of a needle, millions of men, women, and children were hungry and being trampled by commercial monsters—and the church remained silent.

Indeed, we can readily see that theology and church politics have often appeared blind to the deep needs of mankind. And a part of us goes out to the critic, even the Marxist atheist, who sees the sham which is frequently found in the Christian church. It would appear that it is this element of sensitivity, found in the humble Christian as well as the honest Marxist, which might serve as a contact point with Marxist atheism, for the Marxist too be-

76

lieves that man must come of age, must assume greater responsibility for his fellowman.

Of course, this is not to ignore the fact that the Christian faith and Marxist atheism are at odds in just about every way. It is only to say that they may not be completely and absolutely out of each other's sight. When Marxists claim that evil must be eradicated and that much evil finds its genesis in man's exploitation of man, the Christian must agree. And when Marxists assert that truth can best be known through living interaction with the real world, sensitive Christians must sense a similar foothold. Such agreement does point up a splinter of hope and a single, if admittedly minute, flame which can perhaps warm the hands of both camps.

SUMMARY

Marxist atheism is today a political force of great magnitude. Though world communism is complex and dynamic, it manifests several basic propensities: (1) it is decidedly dogmatic in theory and in practice; (2) it believes that its major assertions are firmly grounded in modern science; (3) it is invariably and especially antichristian; (4) it is convinced that man must be the supreme being for man; and (5) it is existential in practice; that is, it demands total commitment to its truth.

Because modern communism requires absolute loyalty to its teachings, religion cannot possibly find a place in its circle, and this is true because religion often includes a private dimension which cannot be tolerated by a closed system and because religion, especially Christianity, acknowledges a Power beyond man, a Power which in some mysterious way helps to determine man's destiny.

Much of communism, though antichristian, is no longer openly militant in its attitude toward churches, being convinced that religion will fade away under its own corroding errors.

Christians who believe that Marxist atheism is unnatural forget that many of the same needs met by traditional religion are met by contemporary communism and that a natural "return to religion" is in no way guaranteed.

There appears to be no way of honestly bridging the gap between Marxist atheism and the Christian faith except the faint but persistent hope that both systems of belief and commitment agree that evil must be rooted out wherever it is found in the world and that to do this man must learn to live in harmony and goodwill.

quote : Karl May
Pg. 59

4. Christian Atheism

God is dethroned; and although the incognizant masses are tardy in realizing the event, they feel the icy draught caused by that vacancy. Man enters upon a spiritual ice age; the established churches can no longer provide more than Eskimo huts where their shivering flock huddles together.
—Arthur Koestler

The Christian layman does not find it especially difficult to understand why and how a Communist can embrace unbelief. But there does appear to be something strangely wrong about the phrase "Christian atheist." Is this not a contradiction in terms, a monstrous play on words, or worse still, a dishonest and unforgivable bit of theological gobbledygook? How is it possible, we want to know, for the Christian to argue that God is no longer, if indeed he ever was, a personal force in our lives, sustaining us in his infinite love?

Such a question is difficult to answer, and for several reasons, not the least of which is the fact that the phrase "death of God" means many things to many people. Two of the most popular death-of-

79

God theologians remind us that the phrase can mean at least ten different things:

1. That there is no God and that there never has been. This position is traditional atheism of the old-fashioned kind, and it does seem hard to see how it could be combined, except very unstably, with Christianity or any of the Western religions.

2. That there once was a God to whom adoration, praise and trust were appropriate, possible, and even necessary, but that now there is no such God. This is the position of the death of God or radical theology. It is an atheist position, but with a difference. If there was a God, and if there now isn't, it should be possible to indicate why this change took place, when it took place, and who was responsible for it.

3. That the idea of God and the word God itself are in need of radical reformulation. Perhaps totally new words are needed; perhaps a decent silence about God should be observed; but ultimately, a new treatment of the idea and the word can be expected, however unexpected and surprising it may turn out to be.

4. That our traditional liturgical and theological language needs a thorough overhaul; the reality abides, but classical modes of thought and forms of language may well have had it.

5. That the Christian story is no longer a saving or a healing story. It may manage to stay on as merely illuminating or instructing or guiding, but it no longer performs its classical functions of salvation or redemption. In this new form, it might help us cope with the demons, but it cannot abolish them.

80

6. That certain concepts of God, often in the past confused with the classical Christian doctrine of God, must be destroyed: for example, God as problem solver, absolute power, necessary being, the object of ultimate concern.

7. That men do not today experience God except as hidden, absent, silent. We live, so to speak, in the time of the death of God, though that time will doubtless pass.

8. That the gods men make, in their thought and action (false gods or idols, in other words), must always die so that the true object of thought and action, the true God, might emerge, come to life, to born anew.

9. That of a mystical meaning: God must die in the world so that he can be born in us. In many forms of mysticism the death of Jesus on the cross is the time of that worldly death. This is a medieval idea that influenced Martin Luther, and it is probably this complex of ideas that lies behind the German chorale "God Himself is Dead" that may well be the historical source for our modern use of "death of God."

10. Finally, that our language about God is always inadequate and imperfect.[1]

Every Christian layman who enters the contemporary radical theology dialogue ought to be aware of these ten possible meanings of the phrase "God is dead." He ought also be aware that not one of these meanings is radically new in the sense that it was

[1] From *Radical Theology and the Death of God*, copyright © 1966 by Thomas J. J. Altizer and William Hamilton, reprinted by permission of the publishers, The Bobbs-Merrill Company, Inc.

formulated for the first time in the twentieth century. Indeed, it would appear nearly impossible to come up with a startling brand-new theological idea. In this respect professional theologians of the past were ingenuous thinkers. Often students of theology, hoping to startle their professors with a "new" idea, soon discover that someone a long time ago wrote several volumes on the very same subject. Though such experiences are not always good for the ego, they can in time lead to a kind of humility which brings the scholar closer to the reality of the theological as well as the secular worlds.

Unfortunately, laymen often pick up bits and pieces of information which sound radical and novel. They may not know much about theology, perhaps not even care much about it; but when they hear someone say "God is dead," they get excited, angry, or perhaps even defensive.

A few years ago a pastor friend of mine told me that one of his members came rushing into his study waving a copy of a national magazine over her head. She shouted, "This says God is dead. And one of our seminaries is teaching that God is dead!" My friend answered, "What should surprise you about the death of God? Most of you in this parish have been living for the past ten years as if you already had accepted that event!"

Later when this pastor reflected on his own spontaneous and regretful reaction, he saw that part of his own anger stemmed from the realization that the phrase, very old to him, had got life from a national magazine, and now he like thousands of other pastors would need to teach the danger of catch phrases and stark oversimplifications. What was perhaps just as disturbing was the knowledge that this laywoman would not read or study anything beyond the national magazine. Only the phrase "God is dead" would remain with her, coloring, undoubtedly, her attitude toward the university in question and the denominational leadership "which would let such a radical thought get started."

Of course, there is no need for such situations to develop if we can retain a perspective wide enough and cautious enough to permit us to remember always that God's world is indeed *his*, and it is of *his* magnitude. Since we are finite creatures, we must know that our limitations are just that—limitations. This does not stop us from searching and questioning what others say about God and faith. It is equally important that a truly Christian perspective should lead us to say, "Yes, the idea that God is dead is an interesting idea. I shall try to discover how or why it came about, and certainly I shall test it against my own life and experiences. Then perhaps I shall have something intelligent to say about it."

BACKGROUND OF THE GOD-IS-DEAD IDEA

With this intention in mind we might profitably consider the background of the popular phrase

"God is dead," for as we have noted, it can mean many things. But to the Christian it often sounds like a radical and unmistakable atheistic statement.

Yet there is one way in which the phrase has been used which does not necessarily imply literal atheism. Martin Luther, the father and leader of the Protestant Reformation, often said, "God himself is dead." Indeed, many of us have sung the chorale containing these very words. In this sense, what happened on Calvary had to do with the death of God. At that time and place man killed God.

Or at some time later in history philosophers and theologians spoke of the death of the "abstract God," meaning that the Christian must experience the death of this abstract God before he can know the true, living, concrete God. Few of us would argue with this use of the phrase. We most certainly know that the God of the sophisticated philosopher is not the God of our inner faith!

Undoubtedly it is the German philosopher Friedrich Nietzsche's (1844-1900) use of the phrase "God is dead" that offers most to us in our search for understanding today's emphasis on radical theology. Nietzsche's influence on the world has been phenomenal. A severe critic of Christianity, most of his resentment and analysis of the faith still serve as bedrock for contemporary attacks on Christianity.

Nietzsche explained religion in terms of the unconscious process of projection. Man, insisted Nietzsche, at times becomes aware of the power which slumbers within him. Also, he at great moments senses the love he is capable of giving. But he fears assigning this superhuman quality to himself. He creates, in other words, two worlds out of the two spheres of his own nature. One, the ordinary and weak, he calls man. The other, the rare and good, he calls God.

To this tendency Nietzsche directed all his contempt and disgust. He especially hated Christianity because it not only illustrated the process, it encouraged the distinction between man and God at every opportunity. He once said, "I consider Christianity the most nefarious of seductions and lies. It is the Great Lie and blasphemy par excellence." And he meant it!

For Nietzsche the only hope was that men should kill this God whom they had given such high values. He felt that though it would take centuries for most people to acknowledge the passing of God, it would in time take place. Man, especially thinking man, must continuously and strenuously proclaim the death of God. We must work diligently at the task of wiping from men's minds the very idea of God. Nietzsche's own words are most direct: "We have killed God. The most sacred and powerful force the world has hitherto possessed now bleeds beneath our knife. . . . The grandeur of this act is too great for us. Is it not necessary that, as a result of this act, we become gods ourselves? . . . There has never been a more grandiose act and those who are born after us will belong, because of this act, to a higher history. . . . We are God's assassins." [2]

To the sensitive Christian, he who believes that God's grace does indeed represent the good, such a statement may rub hard. He may well wonder if the contemporary death-of-God theology is cut from the same fabric as Nietzsche's outbursts. Let's see if we can discover any similarities or differences.

MANY DEATH-OF-GOD THEOLOGIES

In the first place, there is no one death-of-God theology. The three leading exponents of what has been called "radical theology" are Thomas J. J. Altizer, William Hamilton, and Paul Van Buren. Yet these three men differ widely in what they mean by Christian atheism. In this section I shall try to summarize briefly some of their primary meanings, realizing that far more elaborate and detailed descriptions are available elsewhere.[3]

We might start by mentioning the fact that in recent years many theologians have observed that old, traditional ideas of God can no longer stand the test of reality. The "old-time religion," especially its view of the nature of God, simply cannot stand up under the contemporary facts of scientific knowledge and general enlightenment. To believe that God is a be-

[2] Quoted in Lepp, *Atheism in Our Time*, p. 168.
[3] Especially helpful is Thomas W. Ogletree's *The Death of God Controversy* (Nashville: Abingdon Press, 1966).

86

nevolent old man, perhaps with a long white beard, and that he watches over us, parceling out rewards and punishments, simply cannot be seriously believed by the modern person. The God who answers our egocentric prayers, who solves our personal, national, and international problems, no longer seriously exists in the minds and lives of most intelligent people. Some few may still cling to this childish idea of God, but such an anthropomorphic concept is not capable of withstanding the onslaughts of modern knowledge about the universe, its developmental nature, and its operation.

This kind of God has passed from the minds of men. This is a cultural fact. And this passing can be described as the death of God. Of course, it would be more accurate to say the death of a particular kind of God. Nevertheless, the phrase "death of God" has been used to refer to the cultural fact that the traditional anthropomorphic concept of God is no longer a live opinion. God's death in this sense is indeed a cultural event—something like the disappearance of the trolley car—but the event does not destroy the reality of God himself.

Some Christians hurriedly add that the "real" God is and remains "wholly other," beyond any cultural idea or fact. Such an argument is not difficult to understand. But Christian atheism is something quite more than this. For some radical theologians the death of God is more than a cultural event; it is a theological assertion.

87

As has been said, the modern radical theologians mean different things, and their writings and thoughts reveal many changes and shifts. But one observer of their work notes four similarities which can serve us well in our attempt to touch the core of the death-of-God movement:

(1) the assertion of the unreality of God for our age, including the understandings of God which have been a part of traditional Christian theology; (2) the insistence upon coming to grips with contemporary culture as a necessary feature of responsible theological work; (3) varying degrees and forms of alienation from the church as it is now constituted; and (4) recognition of the centrality of the person of Christ in theological reflection.[4]

Though the radical theologians—the Christian atheists—differ in their interpretations of these points, there is enough common argument for us to use these observations to help us understand what death-of-God theology is all about.

Already we have noted that some of these thinkers assert that our modern age cannot hold to the old and traditional ideas of God. When, for example, the famous theologian Paul Tillich referred to the death of God, he usually meant the loss of the idea of God as a big person. For him the death of God meant the death of idols, those false gods that saturate our culture.

[4] *Ibid.*, p. 26.

88

Or, when, for example, John A. T. Robinson, Bishop of Woolwich, asks the question, "Can a truly contemporary person *not* be an atheist?" he is drawing us into a consideration of the old ideas of God. He writes:

I want to treat the question of atheism as a very serious one for those of us who call ourselves Christians. So I have deliberately posed it, for myself as well as for you, in the form: "Can a truly contemporary person *not* be an atheist?" For I believe there is an important sense in which a person who is fully a man of our times *must*—or, at any rate, *may*—be an atheist before he can be a Christian. That is to say, there is so much in the atheist's case which is true that for many people today the only Christian faith which can be valid *for them* is one that takes over *post mortem dei*, after the death of God as "God" has traditionally been understood.[5]

With the phrase "as God has traditionally been understood" Bishop Robinson tells us what God he is speaking of, and for this we can be thankful. For some modern theologians fail to tell us this important fact. After all, it is still pretty much true that only a fool could say in any final, authoritative way that God is dead. He must explain *what* God is dead or *whose* God is dead.

As a psychologist, for example, I might well conclude, "Ah, 'tis sad; but for many of my counselees

[5] John A. T. Robinson, *The New Reformation?* (Philadelphia: Westminster Press, 1965), p. 106.

God is indeed dead. He is no longer psychologically *real* to them." I believe this to be a very true statement, describing things as they are. God in the mid-twentieth century is simply not *real* in the minds of a growing number of people. When on Sunday morning the preacher says "we must love God," the statement is for many meaningless because God is not perceived as being a living part of their psychological field.

In this sense the psychologist *and* the theologian might well say that God is dead for all practical purposes. But this is a far cry from asserting that God is dead and meaning that he has "died out of existence," so to speak. *The metaphysical meaning, we can well argue, is impossible for finite men to make without playing the part of a fool.*

So our lesson is a simple one: we must learn to require precision from those who make such statements. This observation from Denis de Rougemont might serve us well as we ponder the issue:

Have we ever asked any of those who say that God is dead just what they mean by such an assertion? What God is dead? The God they imagine, or the God about whom so many people pray? A convenient caricature, or the First Person of the Trinity? The God about whom philosophers speculate, or the God whom prophets announce? A psychological attitude, or an ontological reality? . . . To insist upon a little honest clarity would be a way of pointing out to these modern writers a few of the inextricable difficulties into which assertions plunge not only their own but all Western thought.[6]

We do have a right to expect clarity from those who tell us that God is dead. Once we have their meaning, we are in a position to evaluate their arguments in relation to our own thoughts and our own spiritual development.

Another similarity often found in the radical theology literature is the insistence that Christian theology has a responsibility to come to grips with the real world of today. Though death-of-God advocates vary in the emphasis placed on this issue, most demand far more theological *action* than has customarily been the example of much theology in the past.

On this point the Christian layman, who after all must be something of a theologian himself, needs to ponder seriously. The radical theologians have argued again and again that theology has too long played the fiddle while a great world burns; too long has it pulled the shades of its comfortable study while the people in the streets cried for bread or groaned for justice. Theology, argue these critics, has spoken completely and deeply over minutia; it has been preoccupied with a pimple on its nose while in fact it was dying of cancer.

But even more serious than this accusation is the judgment that already it is really too late for theology

[6] Quoted in Martin E. Marty, *Varieties of Unbelief* (Anchor Books ed.; Garden City: Doubleday & Co., 1966), p. 45.

91

to confront contemporary culture seriously and meaningfully. The death of God prophets are saying the collapse of meaning related to God already probably eliminates the "chance" theology has had. For too many years it has refused to face up to the task of finding the relevance of the gospel for contemporary times. Already the totality of human experience has lost the awareness of God and therefore theology, which has God as its datum, has a catch-up function which might well prove to be impossible —a matter of too little and too late.

Is the situation hopeless? Can Christian theology still come to grips with the present world? Or is theology to become a lost science, an intellectual exercise puffing in an attic of dust and past memories? Though here again we find differences in the death-of-God theologies, most hold up some hope. They argue that it is possible for the Christian to move through and beyond the God-is-dead phase of thought. Already we have noted the Bishop of Woolwich's thesis that we must pass beyond the traditional concepts of God. He dramatically asks, "Can a truly contemporary person *not* be an atheist?" Bishop Robinson does not argue that all Christians *must* go through atheism before coming to a genuine Christian faith. He does claim that a growing number of Christians in our kind of world will need to do just this.

Perhaps this is where we will need to leave the issue for the moment, for there is no single answer for everyone. Apparently the death of God is a necessary idea for a growing number of people who seriously yearn for a more meaningful life. For those who have not come to this place and will not come to this place reservation of judgment may be the most Christian stance to take. The same, of course, ought to hold for the radical theologian; he ought to appreciate the truth that for many their God *can and does* survive all the contemporary thrusts which bear in upon a life open to the events of modern times.

Motives for Christian Atheism

Yet this does not settle the issue, nor does it satisfy the believers. After all, the radical theologian often tries to explain away the traditionally faithful. Often he reasons that the believer has personal or social motives for his faith and that these forces account for his belief. At times he offers the psychological explanation claiming that the faithful *need* a trusting Father who watches over them. Or he insists that the traditional Christian has developed a form of "tunnel vision" whereby he refuses to see the cruel facts of this world, perceiving instead only that which he wishes to see.

As true as such explanations may be, motivation is always a two-way street. Motivation is blanket-like in nature. And it is therefore quite right to ask, "Why do radical theologians claim that God is dead?"

"Why do Christian atheists insist that the traditional views of God are no longer valid?" "Why do Christian atheists often demand that all Christians *must* abandon the God of traditional theism?"

We cannot hope to identify all the factors which help to explain the forces behind Christian atheism. But we can, it seems, identify at least five which are at work. First, as we have already noted, the impact of contemporary culture is simply too much for the traditional ideas of Christianity. Scientific world views have made obsolete the biblical stories and events, no matter the ingenious interpretations conjured up by liberal scholars. The fact is that the pervasive view of the world today is considerably different from the views found in the Bible. The average Christian senses these inconsistencies and rather than grapple with them, abandons his traditional faith and finds the phrase "God is dead" a convenient and shorthand way of summing up his dilemma.

Second, the world of suffering and affliction has come home to contemporary man in a way not previously experienced by him. Of course, sensitive men always have been aware of the sheer power of affliction. Hardly a man has lived who has not had suffering touch him in a personal way. But modern communication makes available to man a widened consciousness never before available to the masses. Anyone who is more than a vegetable will be affected by this new and broad awareness of the extent of human suffering. Many such people find this em-

94

pirical fact too much for their faith in a good God.

Third, as we noted in examining Marxist atheism, some men observe in history a religious tyranny which repels them. They see organized religion as the sponsor of many acts and programs designed to rob man of his dignity. We have noted this dynamic in some detail in looking at communist atheism, but we might add that this dynamic works in many persons who are not at all touched by Marxist ideology.

Fourth, the Christian atheist may come to his views by default and neglect. By this is meant that many Christians are atheists *in fact* because they have not worked at their faith. They have drifted along pulling their childish faith behind them. They are indeed Christian atheists by default. (We will need to look a bit more closely at this group in the following chapter where this type of atheism will be called "practical" atheism.)

Fifth and finally, Christian atheism may be the result of psychological processes and emotional cripplings. In chapter five this motive will be examined a bit more carefully, for it is often bound up in the other "more reasonable" explanations. Yet the personal motive can be an important factor in explaining how Christian atheism comes about. The nature of neurotic atheism is complex, but we must keep it in our sight as a real and powerful fact.

The motives for expressing Christian atheism are, then, many and varied. They are, as we have seen, quite similar to the causes behind Marxist atheism.

95

But we need to ask the question, "Are there genuine differences?"

CHRISTIAN ATHEISM AND
OTHER FORMS OF ATHEISM

When we compare classical atheism and Marxist atheism with Christian atheism, we can find many similarities. Much of contemporary atheism, including Christian atheism, tends to lay great stress on man's responsibility in a seemingly meaningless world. Many atheists agree that Christianity has not demanded enough of man, or, put another way, man is basically far better than ordinary Christianity seems to picture him. There tends to be a point where all contemporary atheistic stances intersect, and this intersection is marked by the general agreement that man ought to be better than he has been while lounging in the shadow of atheism.

But Christian atheists, though they may agree with this point, add a dimension of uniqueness: many radical theologians force us to take seriously the biblical teaching that Christ is present *in the world*. One view of this is that God has emptied himself totally into flesh in the person of Jesus Christ, and it is here and here only where we will find God. In this sense the Word is truly incarnate. Christ is present in the worldly process we see unfolding before us. As we participate in this presence, we do what is

Christian, and we move beyond God-is-dead theology.

We might well ask how the presence of Christ is made known to us. Again, remembering the differences which exist among radical theologians, we can sample a meaning which might help us understand the place of Jesus in the death-of-God discussion. In one of his books William Hamilton traces the various titles given to Jesus in the New Testament, such as Christ, Son of God, Son of man, and so forth. He finally concludes that "Lord" is the most accurate designation *if* we mean by the lordship of Jesus a lordship of suffering and humiliation. Dr. Hamilton even argues that it is indeed correct to speak of the divinity of Jesus if we understand divinity to mean humiliation. He writes:

In Jesus the Lord we see for the first time what Christian "divinity" must be taken to be: it is God withdrawing from all claims to power and authority and sovereignty, and consenting to become himself the victim and subject of all that the world can do. The afflicting God . . . becomes now the afflicted God. Divinity in Jesus is not withdrawal from the world; it is full consent to abide in the world, and to allow the world to have its way with it.[7]

What this means for the individual Christian is a stark and terrifying possibility. Dr. Hamilton asks, "How can we do the will of God without destroying

[7] *The New Essence of Christianity* (New York: Association Press, 1961), pp. 90-91.

97

ourselves both professionally and personally?" This is the agonizing question every Christian must face. Some death-of-God theologians find the answer in the person of Christ, in a Christian style of life which requires Christ as an example.

In the last chapter of this book we will want to look a bit more closely at what this Christian style of life means. Here we wish only to note that Christian atheism differs from Marxist atheism in that it frequently finds man's hope in a new understanding of Jesus and in his presence in this world here and now.

SUMMARY

Often radical theology is characterized by the catch phrase "God is dead." Yet the phrase can mean many things and has meant many things in the history of ideas. Nietzsche's use of the phrase was negative and final; for him, man has killed God and now can get on with things. But most of the contemporary death-of-God theologians mean something different from this. They argue instead that the "wholly other" concept of God must pass away since it cannot deal effectively with contemporary culture.

The Christian layman has a right to know what is meant when the phrase "God is dead" is used by Christian writers and theologians. After all, there is a difference between saying that a certain concept of God is dead and insisting that the metaphysical God is dead.

Motives for insisting that God is dead include the belief that the realities of our modern day cannot be truly understood by a traditional idea of God, that the world of suffering and affliction simply rules out a benevolent Father God who watches patiently over his children, that the typical history of organized religion makes it suspect and even basically evil in nature, that a drifting materialism and socialism have demonstrated Christianity to be unnecessary, and that certain individual psychological processes may lend themselves to the denial of God.

There appears to be one basic difference between much of Christian atheism and much of classical and Marxism atheism: it is the assertion that passing beyond the death of God can lead to a fresh understanding of Christ's presence in the world, and that sharing in this presence is the individual Christian's cross, his opportunity, and his hope.

5. Unconscious Atheism

*"Then, father," he [Dives] replied, "will you
send him to my father's house, where I have five
brothers, to warn them, so that they too may not
come to this place of torment?" But Abraham said,
"They have Moses and the prophets; let them listen
to them." "No, father Abraham," he replied, "but
if someone from the dead visits them, they will
repent." Abraham answered, "If they do not listen
to Moses and the prophets they will pay no heed
even if someone should rise from the dead."*
—Luke 16:26-31 (NEB)

Marxist and Christian atheism are rational
systems of thought. Though they are not devoid of an
emotional dimension, up to this point in our study
we have tended to look at them in terms of programs
of thought developed by men in a conscious way.
For didactic purposes it is necessary to consider contemporary atheism in this fashion. But as I tried to
show in chapter two, the psychological and emotional
roots of modern atheism are real and vital. Pure
thoughts and pure emotions are abstractions. No
thought is free-floating, devoid of feeling tone. And
every emotional response has thought content.
In this chapter I should like to draw attention to

100

two forms of atheism which are not, strictly speaking, consciously intended types. Instead, they come about because of personal factors of a psychological nature. Without falling into the trap of psychologism, we shall consider the two forms of "unconscious" atheism as very important kinds of contemporary atheism.

First, I shall try to make a distinction between conscious atheism and unconscious atheism. Then I shall describe one type of unconscious atheism under the category "neurotic" atheism and the second type under the name "practical" atheism. Finally it will be argued that modern idolatry influences and nurtures both kinds of unconscious atheism.

Conscious and Unconscious Atheism

Let's start the consideration of the differences between conscious atheism and unconscious atheism by admitting that the extremes are hardly ever found. This may be a disquieting fact since we all like to have neat boxes in which to keep our thoughts and ideas. But in light of what we know about the human mind such an observation appears closer to the truth than would the belief that the conscious/unconscious division can be sliced cleanly and conspicuously. The fact seems to be that there is a psychological continuum ranging from complete unawareness to acute awareness. The average person moves up and down this continuum like an elevator moves from the basement to the penthouse in an apartment building.

In this line of thinking, conscious intention is a matter of degree, not of exclusiveness. Yet if the apartment building has ten floors, the top one is the highest, and the basement is the lowest, and the fifth floor is the middle. Transferring our figure to that of the human mind, the psyche, we can say that the fifth floor represents neither pure consciousness nor pure unconsciousness. It is somewhere in between, partly conscious and partly unconscious. Most of us live somewhere around the fifth floor. But there are those—sometimes called neurotics—who live most of the time in the basement or on the second or third floors. They very often find atheism a sort of therapy or at least a system apparently pleasantly suited to their particular needs.

But before turning to them we ought to recognize those individuals who live at least most of the time on one or more of the upper floors. These people are characterized by a high degree of conscious intention. That is, they face the world rather realistically, are aware of its positive as well as its negative aspects, and have learned to deal with the world and themselves in a way which brings satisfaction. They are, generally speaking, aware of the inner and outer worlds and have learned to cope with both in creative and healthy ways.

In fact, these fortunate people are often called mature or emotionally well adjusted. No matter how they are labeled, they have learned usually from childhood up to deal with life in a successful way, and though they may have their ups and downs, they usually land on their feet and are not overpowered or crushed by the circumstances of life.

Such people may, in developing their general outlook on life, come to atheism in a rather direct, consciously precise way. Through careful analysis, coupled with intense study and critical examination, they may conclude that either Marxist atheism or Christian atheism is a fruitful, truthful, and genuine world view. It is through examination and critical judgment that they come to embrace some sort of atheistic stance.

Forgetting for the moment that pure conscious intending is never perfectly free of unconscious motives, we may say that these people arrive at their position of atheism under the force and genius of a conscious mind devoted to the vigorous task of carving out a world from the raw materials of life.

We have met the fruits of the thoughts of some of these people in previous chapters. Now, however, we want to pay attention to two sorts of unconscious atheism which need to be recognized and appreciated. The first is neurotic atheism. The second is practical atheism.

NEUROTIC ATHEISM

Some psychiatrists and psychologists have characterized neurotic unbelief as differing from sane unbelief in that neurotic unbelief is irrational and excessive in character. Neurotic atheism, in other words, is a form of unbelief motivated by unconscious forces and manifesting itself in extreme ways.

But the difference is in need of further elaboration. Such elaboration might profitably begin by recognizing the common core of what we have come to call neuroticism. Unfortunately, we have come to use the word "neurotic" glibly at times. It is not unusual to hear the phrases, "She's neurotic, of course," or "How neurotic can you get?" when people observe behavior which appears to them to be odd or irrational. Of course, we might well expect, neuroticism is far more complex a condition than our everyday use of the term would indicate. Before me, for example, is a recent volume completely dedicated to explaining the neuroses. It is 1076 pages long! And if there is a central theme to this titanic volume, it is that the neuroses have one thing in common: they originate in anxiety.[1]

And what is anxiety? The author of this exhaustive study says that anxiety is *"the apprehensive tension or uneasiness which stems from the subjective anticipation of imminent or impending danger, in which the source is largely unknown or unrecognized."* [2] There are many theories to explain how this condition originates, but an examination of these explanations

[1] Henry P. Laughlin, *The Neuroses* (Washington: Butterworths, 1967).
[2] *Ibid.*, p. 11.

104

would take us too far afield. Here we wish only to recognize that anxiety is widespread, claiming all of us at some time or other, and that there are many people who suffer so intensely from anxiety that they cannot adequately cope with the world. These people in time become neurotic.

We readily see an example of neurotic behavior in the case of Lisa, briefly presented in chapter two. Rereading that account may help us see the results of a basically neurotic orientation as it uses atheism in its plight.

But perhaps a personal account will help clarify the nature of anxiety, neuroticism, and neurotic atheism. The day following Russia's successful launching of Sputnik, a young lady—let's call her Betty—came knocking on my door late one evening; it was nearly midnight. I knew Betty to be a bright college senior, a chemistry major. She was attractive in a boyish way, extremely articulate, and destined, I imagined, for a brilliant career in science. Her story went something like this: "The Russians have beat us into space. This is the end of everything, I'm sure. For weeks I felt that something awful was going to happen, and now it has. All my beliefs are gone. If there were a God, he would not let such a terrible thing happen. The materialistic Communists have beaten us. There's nothing left. Nothing!"

Of course, I cannot in this brief account show the great and sincere turmoil this young lady presented in her speech. She wept while she went over her story.

And she obviously believed that total destruction was upon us all, to the point that she seriously questioned the wisdom of completing her college work. Her faith was gone. She was, she said, a complete atheist, although she had been reared in a Christian home by devout parents.

During the next several months I saw Betty regularly. Though I convinced her that she ought to stick with her studies, her academic work nevertheless deteriorated. She explained this with the belief that it didn't matter anyway. All scientific advancement was now in the hands of the Russians. What was the use of pretending?

And, of course, she stopped going to church. Indeed, her verbal attacks against the church were frequent and violent. Nothing was sacred anymore. For the first time in her life she discovered Nietzsche and Camus; she read their books and from them found much articulate ammunition for her new, critical, and verbal cannons.

However, after several weeks of counseling Betty began to talk about some personal matters. At first these concerns were almost parenthetical, hardly worth mentioning. There was, for example, the problem of Chuck, her boyfriend, doing graduate work in an out-of-state university. His letters, once passionate and frequent, were growing cool and intermittent. The two young people had a "perfect understanding" worked out rationally "as two young scientists in the twentieth century ought to work out such things." And there were problems with her parents, both of whom felt that Betty was just a bit too free with herself. They simply didn't trust her, especially when she traveled for weekend visits with Chuck.

Thus it was that the personal problems began to appear; and soon Sputnik, science, and atheism were heard less and less until finally, after several months of counseling, Betty faced the issues of her relationships with her parents and with her boyfriend. In time she cut loose from her parents, and she broke off with Chuck. She returned to her studies, completed her undergraduate and graduate degrees, met and married an engineer, and is now taking care of two youngsters and teaching high school chemistry as a substitute teacher. And I doubt if she calls herself an atheist anymore.

Of course, there is not another "case" exactly like Betty's, but she does, I believe, illustrate some of the psychological dynamics of neurotic atheism. Let's see if we can state them directly, using Betty to back up the generalizations.

First, neurotic atheism has its roots in irrational or unconscious conditions. In the case of Betty these unconscious conditions were complex but included faulty relationships with parents and lover.

Second, neurotic atheism is often exaggerated and reactionary. During Betty's period of atheistic arguments, she violently opposed all Christian beliefs, seeking out the most devastating kind of rationalizations to support her new views.

Third, neurotic atheism has its being in anxiety, that dreadful kind of fear which seems to have no real point of reference. Betty's anxiety was spawned by many faulty interpersonal relationships, but she quietly converted it into a specific fear, in this case, the scientific superiority of the USSR as dramatically illustrated in that country's space program.

Fourth, neurotic atheism is contentwise no different from nonneurotic atheism. Betty used the same words, symbols, and arguments used by any other atheist.

Though it must be admitted that neurotic atheism is often more subtle than we find it in the case of Betty, it is nevertheless identifiable by the presence of these four major characteristics.

Just how much of contemporary atheism may be called neurotic is surely a moot question. That a significant number of people are neurotic atheists seems evident. Perhaps, indeed, only the practical atheist surpasses him in population.

Practical Atheism

Practical atheism is used here to describe a form of unbelief which is characterized by drift and apathy. It refers to that very large group of people who would never admit to being atheist but who nevertheless live their individual lives without any meaningful reference to God. In a sense practical atheism is unconscious atheism though it is not necessarily neurotic atheism.

When, for example, the minister told his parishioner that she ought not be shocked or surprised to learn of the death of God since she had been *living as if* God were dead all along, we see a reference to practical atheism. Indeed, when preachers talk about atheism from the pulpit, they invariably are making reference to practical atheism. In fact, it appears almost impossible to discuss the subject of practical atheism without resorting to preaching. For practical atheism, no matter what else it may be, implies a judgment on how functional another's verbalized beliefs appear to be.

To be more specific and to hold to the way in which we tried to understand neurotic atheism, let's turn to the life of a particular individual. In this instance we'll draw on a character taken from American literature—George F. Babbitt, the real estate broker in Sinclair Lewis' book *Babbitt*. This is the way Lewis depicts George Babbitt's religion:

Actually, the content of his theology was that there was a supreme being who had tried to make us perfect, but presumably had failed; that if one was a Good Man he would go to a place called Heaven (Babbitt unconsciously pictures it as rather like an excellent hotel with a private garden), but if one was a Bad Man, that is, if he murdered or committed burglary or used cocaine or had mistresses or sold non-existent real estate, he would be punished. Babbitt was uncertain, however, about what he called "this business of Hell." He explained to Ted, "Of course I'm pretty liberal; I don't exactly believe in a fire-and-brimstone Hell. Stands to reason, though, that a fellow can't get away with all sorts of Vice and not get nicked for it, see how I mean?"

Upon this theology he rarely pondered. The kernel of his practical religion was that it was respectable, and beneficial to one's business to be seen going to services; that the church kept the Worst Elements from being still worse; and that the pastor's sermons, however dull they might seem at the time of taking, yet had a voodooistic power which "did a fellow good—kept him in touch with Higher Things." [3]

As can be seen, Mr. Babbitt expressed belief in a God, but his life as judged from a certain perspective did not appear to demonstrate such a belief. Or to further dramatize the dichotomy, let's read the meaning of Christianity as described by the German Christian Dietrich Bonhoeffer, keeping in mind Babbitt's personal theology:

If our Christianity has ceased to be serious about discipleship, if we have watered down the gospel into emotional uplift which makes no costly demands and which fails to distinguish between natural and Christian existence, then we cannot help regarding the cross as an ordinary everyday calamity, as one of the trials and tribulations of life. We have then forgotten that the cross means rejection and

[3] Sinclair Lewis, *Babbitt* (New York: Harcourt, Brace, 1922), pp. 207-8.

110

shame as well as suffering. The Psalmist was lamenting that he was despised and rejected of men, and that is an essential quality of the suffering of the cross. But this notion has ceased to be intelligible to a Christianity which can no longer see any difference between an ordinary human life and a life committed to Christ. The cross means sharing the suffering of Christ to the last and to the fullest.[4]

Is the comparison between Babbitt's views and Bonhoeffer's views unfair? Have I really set up a pair of straw men in order to make a point? Only partly so in that it is necessary to acknowledge where one stands when defining practical atheism. There *is* a value judgment required. If Dietrich Bonhoeffer's view of Christianity is accepted, then it does not appear difficult to conclude that Babbitt, for all legitimate purposes, was a practical atheist.

But practical atheism is even more complex and insidious than this, for besides including the Babbitts of the world it includes those multitudes of persons who simply do not find it necessary to make any reference at all to God in their lives. Their faith, so to speak, simply does not inform their lives in any significant way. They live their lives not in a hostile stance toward religion, but in a kind of apathetic indifference toward it.

In America, for example, it is rather difficult to find individuals who claim atheism as their position.

[4] Dietrich Bonhoeffer, *The Cost of Discipleship* (New York: The Macmillan Co., 1959), p. 78.

Survey after survey yields only a scant one percent of the population willing to label itself atheistic. Yet observers of the American scene have pointed out that atheism is present; it is a more practical, under-cover kind than that found in modern Europe. It is often subtle, temporary, and unreflective.

Subtle, temporary, unreflective—these are the characteristics which make this type of atheism appear different from the conscious and intentional kinds and even different from the neurotic type, which is frequently violent and excessive. Practical atheism is quiet and unrepulsive, for it is simply, religiously speaking, a synonym for apathy. The practical atheist is, somewhat like certain groups of Marxist atheists, indifferent or immune to the religious question. He is able, if only until the blows of life shock him awake, to wade within the Christian lagoon without letting it dampen his secular trousers. And in this sense practical atheism is unconscious.

ATHEISM AND IDOLATRY

Before concluding our look at these two kinds of unconscious atheism, it should be noted that these rather unreflective types of unbelief appear to be nurtured especially well in the presence of an abundant system of idols. An idol in this case is a material symbol of that which is held to be of supreme value. Though it is most certainly true that from the beginning of history idols have played a major role in man's spiritual quest, contemporary life provides especially rich and multitudinous objects to fill the gap left by the absence of a divinity.

By this I mean that modern times—especially in much of the West—are so filled with materialistic values and pleasurable circumstances that idolatry becomes a very easy pastime. If, for example, we re-read Bonhoeffer's words on the place of the cross in the life of the Christian, we can see how natural and easy it would be to find another object of devotion: money, success, prestige, knowledge, and so forth. These values are at hand and are shared by the many. They become what is ultimately important, and in this sense they generate practical atheism in a vigorous, if subtle, fashion.

As warned, seriously considering unconscious atheism brings with it judgments, evaluations, even homiletical outbursts—all of which have been practiced by the church and individual Christians for the past two thousand years.

Just how the church and the individual Christian have and might confront atheists of all kinds will be the subject of the last two chapters of our study.

SUMMARY

There are two major forms of unconscious atheism: neurotic and practical.

Neurotic atheism is characterized by its irrational and excessive nature. It has its roots in unconscious emotional dynamics, getting its drive from the satisfaction of various needs. Though it is irrational and unconscious, its outer garb often appears the same as other forms of atheism which have their existence in rational, intentional, and reflective processes.

Practical atheism is a form of unbelief characterized by apathy and indifference. The practical atheist sometimes claims a faith, but this faith simply does not play a part in his life. To be identified and named, practical atheism requires an evaluative frame of reference, a point at which we can see the inconsistency between verbalized beliefs and observed behavior.

Unconscious atheism whether neurotic or practical springs up well and easily in times when substitute objects, idols, are readily available for worship and devotion.

PART III

Answers to Atheism

6. *The Church's Answer to Atheism*

━━━━━━━━━━━━━━━━━━

The Church is most true to its own nature when it seeks nothing for itself, renounces power, humbly bears witness to the truth but makes no claim to be the possessor of truth, and is continually dying in order that it may live.

—J. H. Oldham

The summary of atheism presented in previous chapters contains very little which the church has not heard before. Indeed, the church's theologians, ecclesiastical leadership, and various councils have answered such atheistic claims for nearly two thousand years. As an institution and an organization the church has had as one of its functions the answering of propositions which deny God. It has carried out this task in many ways, from official pronouncements to the burning of books and people, from quiet monastic witnessing to the learned arguments of clever theologians.

It is far beyond the scope of this little volume to trace systematically the types and nature of the answers to atheism given by official Christendom during

117

the past two thousand years. That the church has continuously reacted and responded to atheistic talk as part of its war with heresy is a fact of church history. Even modern Christian atheism is beginning to attract the attention of church authorities. The papacy, for instance, recently created an office to deal exclusively with the problem of effective confrontation with contemporary atheism and secularism. And when recent conversations about the death of God hit the popular press, the College of Bishops of The Methodist Church's southeastern jurisdiction found it necessary to prepare a pamphlet calling such radical theologies "pure fantasy, unsupported by any responsible scientific or theological knowledge, and contradicted by the long experience of man on the earth and by unnumbered millions who in the present know the Almighty as the living God."[1]

No matter what we may think of the good bishops' response, it does represent and illustrate a long and accepted way of answering atheistic arguments—through official, rational, and carefully worded documents. Indeed, at the obvious risk of overgeneralizing, it is probably true to say that one of the Christian church's salient answers to atheism has been in the form of rational argument, especially in its many attempts to prove the existence of God.

We will need to look briefly at some distinguished samples of such proofs, examine soberly the nature

---

[1] Quoted in J. Claude Evans, "Tilting at Altizer," *The Christian Century* (March 30, 1966), pp. 391-92.

of such rational arguments, try to understand the contemporary church's reaction to the modern God-is-dead movement, and finally recognize—and I trust appreciate—the church's ideal witness as it confronts current atheism in all its forms.

PROOFS OF GOD'S EXISTENCE

Thinking men have been trying to prove the existence of God for thousands of years. Philosophers and theologians have devised many and often complex arguments to prove that God does indeed exist. Perhaps one of the most famous of proofs is known as the ontological argument, first made respectable by St. Anselm of Canterbury, a great medieval theologian.

Anselm's argument goes something like this: God is the most perfect being conceivable. Then he asks, "Does the most perfect being conceivable exist?" The most perfect being conceivable must exist; otherwise there would be conceivable a more perfect being with all the perfections of the nonexisting one and in addition perfect being. Thus it is, reasoned Anselm, God does indeed exist.

The essence of Anselm's "proof" is that the existence of God follows necessarily from the idea of God. God is a being greater than any being that can be conceived, and a being which exists in fact is greater than one that exists only in thought.

How many books, tracts, sermons, and articles have

119

been written on and about Anselm's ontological argument would be difficult to imagine. Even today in philosophy classes and in theological schools the "proof" is offered. I have even heard it proposed and vigorously defended by college sophomores who have never heard of Anselm or the ontological argument, for the proof has seeped into the folk explanations for God's existence.

Of course, subsequent arguments have demonstrated the fallacy of the medieval theologian's proof. Even St. Thomas Aquinas, genius of Christian theological reasoning, pointed up the error in Anselm's logic. Indeed, it was St. Thomas who furnished us with some of the most penetrating proofs of God's existence. In fact, practically every argument formulated by the church to confront atheism has elements of St. Thomas' thought. It might do us well, therefore, to take a summary glance at this great theologian's five demonstrations proving the existence of God.

The first proof is based on the idea of *motion*. It is necessary to show that God is not only the total cause for all things, but that his continued support is necessary. The proof from motion, therefore, must show that everything depends on God, not simply for a start, but for continuance in motion or existence. The argument is that for every motion we see, we must look elsewhere for its cause since the motion cannot explain itself. This forces us to conclude, argued St. Thomas, that there must be a being without motion, and this being we call God.

The second proof is based on the notion of *efficient causes*. Aristotle said that the efficient cause is that from which first comes any motion or change. For example, the efficient cause of a painting is the artist. The painting cannot cause itself to come into existence. To cause itself would imply that it could not be and be at the same time. There must be, however, an uncaused cause, and this first cause we call God.

The third proof for the existence of God is built on the fact of *contingency*, the observation that all things depend on other things for their continuous existence. Most would agree that every being is contingent. Such contingency and dependence leads to the conclusion—so the argument runs—that there must be a being who escapes such limitations and who is therefore sufficient unto itself. Such a necessary being is God.

The fourth proof is bound up with the idea of *grades of perfection*. This argument notes that all things possess a characteristic of gradation; that is, they are more or less of this or that. Some people are more honest than other people. Some trees are taller than other trees. But that which is the most in any class is the cause of all in that class. That which is most perfect in the order of being is the cause of all being. This perfect being we call God.

The fifth proof for the existence of God is based on the notion of *order*. As we look about, we observe

121

order in the universe. But order itself is dependent upon a purpose. All order, says this argument, comes about in the context of an intention or a goal. Order does not make itself. It is made by God.

These five famous reasons for believing in the existence of God have been used by the church to answer the claims of atheism. We must admit that the cursory way in which they have been presented here makes them appear a bit ridiculous. I trust, however, that including them, even in such a superficial way, will help us see the nature of rational arguments for the existence of God and that such have played an important role in the church's attempts to answer atheists in every age. Surely such arguments along with others will continue to be used by the official institution when it feels it ought to answer the claims of atheism, no matter the kind and type.

Because such arguments have played and continue to play an important part in the life of the church, we ought to give a bit more attention to the nature of rational arguments against atheism.

The Nature of Rational Arguments

It has only been in relatively recent years that we have come to appreciate the complexity of belief systems. Up until the advent of Freudian psychoanalysis, mankind generally was inclined to believe that philosophies and theologies were the result of pure reason and logical considerations. Man, after all, was seen as a rational animal. As we have said before, pure thoughts are abstractions. But more important still is the growing evidence that beliefs are accepted and rejected in the context of many factors besides the reasoning ability of men.

Global belief systems, for instance, tend to be accepted by an individual when he is ready to accept the belief. By ready we mean that a host of other factors—emotional, psychological, developmental, and so forth—must be present before the rational argument can find a home.

At the risk of grossly oversimplifying this principle, let's go back to Betty's plight, presented in a previous chapter. In her very first interview she admitted to being an atheist. Imagine her being presented with St. Thomas' five proofs for the existence of God at this time in the midst of her anguished turmoil! We do not need the pyramid of social science research on beliefs to guess what effect such an approach would have had. No matter how reasonably or articulately the rational arguments might be presented, Betty was not in the proper condition to appreciate them.

Yet the church as an institution frequently has answered atheism in just such a fashion. Perhaps because rational arguments supported by ecclesiastical authorities are easy to come by, this approach has been used freely and often indiscriminately.

It would appear that rational arguments announced by the church have not been especially effective in truly confronting the atheist. This is not to diminish the importance of constructing intelligent theologies. Rather, it is an attempt to claim that even —and especially—rational arguments must be part of a more comprehensive approach to atheism. The belief itself, in other words, dare not become the primary factor. Instead, it is the *ways* beliefs are communicated which must occupy the church as it faces the growing rise of contemporary atheism. When theology begins to think of itself as of greater significance than persons—as often has been the case—it is doubtful whether anyone is going to be convinced of anything. Certainly atheists are not going to be converted to theism!

If the church wishes to confront modern atheism, it must first of all cease believing that it has an exclusive claim on the truth. For this stance can only build an impasse large enough to make conversations between believers and unbelievers utterly impossible. A contemporary scholar in trying to characterize the church's attitudes toward doubters during the Renaissance writes: "For the Renaissance an atheist was one who could not accept any religious principle shared by all Christian creeds. A Jew, a Mohammedan, a deist was an atheist, and the definition could be narrower: to many Protestants, the Pope was the chief Roman Catholic atheist; to many a Roman Catholic, Canterbury was head of the Anglican atheists." [2]

[2] Don Cameron Allen, *Doubt's Boundless Sea: Skepticism and*

Such an attitude did not end in the Renaissance.
Less than two hundred yards from where I write
these words are Christian laymen many of whom believe these exact same judgments. They are, it must
be admitted, quite ill-equipped to meet contemporary atheism. Indeed, at the risk of sounding pe-
dantic, these Christians are, because of their prejudg-
ments and narrowness, incapable of witnessing to one
of the central truths of the faith: the continuous,
unending search for brotherhood among all men
everywhere.

The church too, or at least large segments of it, is
no longer capable of confronting atheists in a genuine
fashion because of its own self-righteousness, its amal-
gamation with opportunistic cultures, and its lack of
compassion for the afflicted and the destitute.

But there is hope; and there are signs that the
church when it is at its best can successfully confront
modern atheism in all its forms. Let's consider how
this might be done both in general and specific terms.

THE CHURCH AND CONTEMPORARY ATHEISM

Every serious Christian must consider and reflect
on what the church means to him, for it is our personal doctrine of the church which will help to determine how we think the church should answer
contemporary atheism. Certainly it is not my inten-

Faith in the Renaissance (Baltimore: Johns Hopkins Press,
1964), Introduction.

tion in this brief introduction to modern atheism to offer a full-blown doctrine of the church, even if such were in my power to do. However, every individual Christian including this one has the responsibility to ask himself, "What does the church mean to me?" Perhaps the following presentation, despite its lack of theological sophistication, will help in considering how a doctrine of the church can help to answer the question, "How ought the church answer contemporary atheism?"

Some years ago the late Bishop Paul Kern offered twelve affirmations of Christian faith, including the following having to do with the nature of the church: "It asserts the claim of Christ as the Incarnate Word of God to the lordship of all human life. . . . It is His body, the instrument of His active power, the bond of fellowship between all those who accept His lordship." In commenting on this assertion Georgia Harkness, a contemporary theologian and religious author, writes:

To believe in the Church as a Body of Christ means many things. It means that there must be a missionary outreach to carry the gospel to many lands. It means that persons must witness to the gospel in a way that will make it relevant to the business, family, and social life of our day. It means the cancelling of all race distinctions within the Christian fellowship and, as soon as possible, within all community life.

It means better church schools and Christian schools of

higher learning so that the heritage of our faith may be passed on more fully and vitally to oncoming generations and so that adults may understand more accurately the foundations of their faith. It means unremitting efforts to eliminate injustice, poverty, hunger, disease, and ignorance wherever they are found.[3]

The powerful implication here is that there ought to be a transforming relationship between the ultimate ideal of the church and the world of events. Paul put it even more remarkably when he wrote to the Corinthians, "If one member suffers, all suffer together; if one member is honored, all rejoice together" (I Cor. 12:26 RSV).

Such affirmations on the nature of the church are primarily theological and form the bedrock of any consideration of the meaning of the church. The church is indirectly the body of Christ, but it is also a *human* community. And it is an appreciation of this human dimension which can help us understand how and why the church has reacted to atheism.

James M. Gustafson of Yale Divinity School illustrates the human factor of the church by titling his book on this subject *Treasure in Earthen Vessels*. Whatever else the church may be, thinks this sociologist, it is in fact an earthen vessel which God has

[3] Georgia Harkness, *Beliefs That Count* (Nashville: Abingdon Press, 1961), pp. 97-98.

chosen to immerse in the life of the world. Dr. Gustafson does not deny the divine dimensions of the church; he merely points up the many *human* dimensions which constitute its being. For example, he sees the church as manifesting seven different facets, all quite understandable without reference to theological terms:

1. The church is a *human* community, possessing qualities and functions in common with other social institutions.

2. The church is a *natural* community, potentially satisfying all those physical, psychological, and emotional needs peculiar to man.

3. The church is a *political* community, possessing the same kinds of power forces and structures found in any other political organization.

4. The church is a community of *language*, the members held together through the internalization of meanings found in the various documents, symbols, and rites.

5. The church is a community of *interpretation* in that its clergy, historians, and theologians carry on a continuous conversation in hope of making the gospel clear and meaningful to every generation.

6. The church is a community of *memory and understanding* in that it seeks to communicate a common past and a common future to its members.

7. The church is a community of *belief and action* in that its membership is committed to its object of

belief and is impelled to act in the light of their loyalty.[4]

Dr. Gustafson's excellent analysis should point out the complexity of the church as a social institution without reference to its divine dimension. It also reveals why it is that the church frequently is perceived as an authoritarian organization, devoid of human compassion and Christian love. For in the functioning of such a complex and finite human community, all the human frailties of men interact and express themselves. The same power struggles and the same hypocritical gymnastics found in all earthly organizations can be found in the church.

And this institutional complexity automatically leads to a desire to simplify its role, to regress or withdraw from life's arena. These tendencies frequently lead to an authoritarian-moralistic response which is simple in that it operates under a set of black/white labels, but dangerous in that it oversimplifies God's creation.

The church *is* an authority, of course; its revelation, its history, its experiences, its total life require that we recognize its wisdom and authority. But the real authority of the church ought to be of the kind attributed to Jesus when the people said, "He taught them as one who had authority, and not as the scribes" (Mark 1:22 RSV). "Authority" here refers to a form of witnessing—demonstrated love, if you will.

[4] *Treasure in Earthen Vessels* (New York: Harper & Row), 1961.

But any organization having such authority is in danger of communicating its wisdom in an authoritarian manner, and this oversimplifies the power and nature of communication. The authoritarian is naïve in that he assumes that clear statements of belief, perhaps even accompanied by threats, will change all those forces which he refuses to see, let alone deal with.

The history of the Christian church demonstrates this tendency in dealing with unbelievers. Far too often have atheists been persecuted, ignored, or struck with scriptural lines suggesting that they stand outside the human community. In dealing with atheists it is necessary for the church to answer one pointed question: *Is the church at its best as an authoritarian judge or a caring community motivated by Christian love?*

Of course, our individual doctrine of the church will help us answer this question. My doctrine claims that the church is at its best when it is a caring community motivated by Christian love, and it is my belief that it is this kind of church which can best answer contemporary atheism.

Frankly, I am quite aware that these general ideas about the meaning of the church are quite bloodless in themselves. And I must admit that there are many times when the church appears to be nothing more than an archaic institution whose major purpose appears to be the preservation of the irrelevant. Yet this bloodless, cumbersome, pathetic institution has in it a force which can answer contemporary atheism in the only genuine way it can be answered: through the witness of a caring, redemptive fellowship.

Christian love can be communicated through all the channels of the church. Worship, sacraments, education, pastoral care, social witness, redemptive groups—all are vessels of God's grace. And all can and ought to confront modern atheism in a positive and open fashion.

As I write these words, I am reminded that in an hour I am to attend as a new member a meeting of the Commission on Education of my local church. Who are these people? How do I feel about them? How will they receive me, their newest member?

Several of them are related to me in my administrative role; in fact, I am "the boss" of two of them. I hardly know several others. One is a fellow clergyman. There are several housewives.

I might be fearful as I prepare to attend this first meeting. But if this commission is an integral part of the caring fellowship, as I believe it is, I need have no fear of the members, nor they of me. We are part of a larger fellowship. We share intentions. We share values. We ought to be able to work together.

But how far can we go in this fellowship of caring persons? My faith is that such a fellowship can go all the way. Properly formed and under the guidance of the Holy Spirit, it can meet and deal with all that modern times can produce—including atheism. But it can do this only when it is at its best, and its best,

131

I believe, is summarized concisely and beautifully in the words at the head of this chapter: *"The Church is most true to its own nature when it seeks nothing for itself, renounces power, humbly bears witness to the truth but makes no claim to be the possessor of truth, and is continually dying in order that it may live."* [5]

This is the way the church can and ought to answer contemporary atheism. That it has not tended to do so in the past does not mean that it cannot do so now and in the future. Fortunately, there are signs that the modern church is beginning to see the atheistic stance in a way which will allow for open conversation and confrontation in love.

New Answers to Atheism

In recent years the Roman Catholic Church has given growing attention to providing opportunities for confrontation with atheists. When, for example, it recently established the secretariat for unbelievers, it demonstrated in a concrete and positive fashion that it *cared* about the unbelievers. Pope Paul VI made it perfectly clear that the Christian church has no intention of excluding atheists, claiming that for the love of truth, discussion is possible and required. And ecumenism, as Pope John XXIII understood it, *had* to include the atheistic segments of the world.

[5] J. H. Oldham, *Life Is Commitment* (New York: Association Press, 1959), p. 103.

Another contemporary example of how the church is beginning to answer atheism may be found in a dialogue between secular humanists and theists sponsored by Alma College, a Jesuit seminary for theological students. Here priests, laymen, and unbelievers meet in open dialogue, clearing the air for future discussion.[6]

Such examples as these point toward a growing awareness on the part of churchmen that the church can best confront modern atheism through sincere attempts at understanding, rather than with judgmental outbursts against unbelievers, so characteristic in bygone days.

Unfortunately, Protestantism has not always shown the same awareness of the reality of contemporary atheism. Yet it too must be itself and seek understanding through Christian concern and love. For the church's answer to contemporary atheism must be the church itself when it is at its best. Nothing less will do.

"In the present phase of things," writes one student of atheism, "it is up to believers not so much to convert the atheist as to understand him. To do that it will be necessary for us to go out from our own framework of thought, to place ourselves through the charity 'that comprehends all things' within the mentality of non-believers." [7] This is not

---

[6] *Secular Humanism and Christianity: A Confrontation of Values* (Los Gatos, Calif.: Alma College, 1966).

[7] Lepp, "The Church and Atheists," p. 90.

an easy task; but such appears to be the calling of the church and individual Christians in the modern world.

SUMMARY

The church's answer to atheism in the past has varied greatly—from great councils dealing violently with heresy to the quiet guidance of the confessional and the spiritual direction of dedicated priests and pastors. But it has in all of this relied most heavily on rational arguments, including proofs of the existence of God.

Though rational argument continues to hold an important place in the church's confrontation with atheism, the nature of such an approach is simply not powerful or comprehensive enough to successfully answer contemporary atheism. Instead the church must find ways of answering atheism while at the same time being true to its own nature which does not include self-righteousness, opportunistic striving, and compassionless communication. The church must abandon its inclination to confront cultures and subcultures, including atheism, as an authoritarian judge. Instead it ought to communicate and witness to its message in the context of a caring community motivated by Christian love.

Certain signs, such as the establishment of offices formed to deal with atheists and symposia with unbelievers, indicate that the church is beginning to see

that atheism must be answered in a positive way
through the witness of the church and its individual
members. But the life of the church and the lives of
its individual members remain the essential qualities
of any genuine answer to contemporary atheism.

7. *The Christian's Answer to Atheism*

We believing Christians need the same honesty and courage in admitting our own responsibility for the thundering advance of atheism in a world in which for two thousand years the Gospel has been preached. It is because our individual and collective conduct as Christians has so seldom conformed to the evangelical spirit that peoples and individuals, awakened to their dignity by Christianity, believe they must declare themselves its enemy.

—Ignace Lepp

It would be presumptuous and naïve to start this last chapter of our study by claiming that the individual Christian's answer to atheism is the same as the answer given by the church when it is at its best. Though there is a partial truth in such a claim, the facts of history and the facts of our own lives do not permit such a general answer. It may well be true that if the individual Christian is able to make as part of himself the church when it is at its best, he has all the necessary witness needed to answer contemporary atheism.

But as we have seen, the church is hardly ever at its best, and individual Christians are unique and complex, and will through their personal natures demonstrate the most certain of spiritual truths in various and secondary ways. That nagging question previously raised by the death-of-God theologian—how can we do the will of God without destroying ourselves both professionally and personally—returns to haunt us. For as individual Christians, we are faced with this demanding query every day of our lives. We cannot shake the question from our minds. It is a charge built into the very nature of the Christian faith. Not to ask it is to be less than Christian. To ask it and answer it fully is the sin of pride. To ask it and attempt in prayer and humility to find the answer is the Way.

It would do us well in considering that small part of this 'question which has to do with atheism to remember that the earliest name of the followers of Jesus was "those of the Way." Linked to this is the equally important fact that these early disciples were called "those of the Way" not because they shared certain beliefs, but because of the meaning their beliefs had for life as demonstrated by the way they lived.

This is the hint of how the Christian ought to answer contemporary atheism. But such a point will need further discussion and clarification. To accomplish this I have chosen in the following concluding pages to try to suggest the gospel's answer to atheism, to examine what it means to say that the gospel must become our psychology, to define the problem of the

Christian's witness in the modern world, to note how atheism can serve the Christian faith, and to insist that there is a point of intersection between atheist and saint, a point which becomes our only hope.

THE GOSPEL'S ANSWER TO ATHEISM

The opening paragraph of L. Harold DeWolf's *A Theology of the Living Church* has often struck me as one of the most sufficient explanations of the nature of the Christian gospel to be found anywhere:

In the midst of the world's tyranny, oppression and fear a wonderful story once began and spread like wildfire from village to village and from nation to nation. Those who told it called it "the good news" and they were so full of its wonder and gladness that even the sternest commands and hardest punishments of emperors could not stop the telling of it. So revolutionary was their message and its power that guardians of the old order said to one another, "They are turning the world upside down." So they were. By the influence of their faith slaves were freed, cruel oppressors were brought down from their thrones, the poor were assisted, the ill were healed, little children were made to laugh and sing as never before and the timid were enabled to face death with triumphant serenity and even with fierce joy.[1]

We have moved far from this direct, simple, and positive concept of the gospel. Since those early days

[1] (Rev. ed.; New York: Harper & Brothers, 1960) p. 17.

men have organized to say and proclaim far more than the basic gospel obviously meant to the early Christians. To the early church and to the individual Christians in that church, the good news was not so much a doctrine as it was an *act*. People had *changed*. They *cared* about one another. These were the central elements of the gospel.

It is most certainly true that the content of the gospel was important and magnificent in its claims. All of what was happening was the revelation of God to man. God was present to man. The person was offered the incredible opportunity to actually participate in the life of God while still in this world. And such a thing was offered to all men.

If we could transform ourselves back into those early days of Christianity, we might sense that what happened among the people was the essence of the good news. To argue over the question as to whether or not God exists would not be a vital point for these people under the spell of the good news of salvation. God's existence was apparent in the light of what was happening among the people. Slaves were freed, cruelty eliminated, the poor were helped, the sick were made whole, children became happy, and men conquered the fear of death. *This* was the gospel, and this was the answer, the only answer, to atheism.

And it must remain so today. The gospel answers atheism in a very unsophisticated way. It does so with the simple acts of persons who claim that what is done is done by the grace of their God. Christians

139

came to see that they were the instruments through whom God's truth was to be made known in the world. Such a faith answers all doubt with lives lived in the spirit of Christ. Any other answer to unbelief would be shabby compared with the gospel's central message, which is that Christ's coming to the world is the focal point of God's plan for the salvation of man.

But these words as powerful as they are do not represent the real gospel, since its central meaning must be found in the lives of persons. The gospel's answer to atheism is embedded in the gospel itself, and this gospel must find its way into the minds of persons before it can meet unbelief in a positive way. Theology, in other words, must become psychology. The gospel must be personified in you and in me before it can become an effective confrontation to modern unbelief. Just as God revealed himself to man through Christ, so we must witness to the truth of the good news through our personal lives.

THEOLOGY BECOMES PSYCHOLOGY

What is meant by the phrase, our theology must become our psychology?

If the gospel itself contains the individual Christian's answer to atheism, how shall it be made real, alive, and impressive in the world? There is only one way; it must become part of a person's very being, including his experience and behavior.

Making our theology—what we believe about God

140

and Christ—our psychology means that we must internalize beliefs in such a way that they will be as much a part of us as are our very bodies.

We might stand a better chance of appreciating the importance of making our theology our psychology if we review briefly the meaning of the word "incarnation," so significant in the life of the Christian faith. The essence of the Christian faith is that God has become man in Jesus Christ in order to bridge the gap which man formed through his revolt. God became man in order to save him. The incarnation is the process of translating God into human form. Since men cannot understand God as God, God must translate himself into those terms which man can understand.

In the same way we can see how necessary it is to translate the spiritual truths of the gospel into human terms if they are to be made meaningful before the world, including the world of the unbeliever. We may, for instance, have some highly sophisticated arguments and convictions about the brotherhood of men, but if this idea has not been made part of us to the extent that we treat others in a brotherly fashion, the Truth has not been made flesh in us; that is, the theological truth remains on a level above the day-by-day affairs of men. It has not become our psychology and is, therefore, a sham. "As we seek to bring people into the fellowship of the gospel," writes one religious leader, "we must not forget that we ourselves are the objects of this gospel and that its grace and power must be evidenced in us. Can it be that persons see so little difference between believers and nonbelievers that they see little advantage in joining us?" [2]

This is what I mean when I claim that the Christian has the task of translating his theology into his psychology. Only then, it seems certain, do we possess the kind of grace and power required to meet the contemporary onslaughts of atheism in all its forms.

THE NATURE OF THE CHRISTIAN WITNESS

This brings us to the important question of the nature of the individual Christian's witness before the ground swell of contemporary atheism. How does he meet the arguments we have examined in previous chapters?

At this point there is a temptation to outline a set of characteristics which might best depict the Christian who has internalized his faith. But such an exercise, already attempted by many, oversimplifies the nature of the incarnation process. When the gospel is translated into personal acts, it loses something in the translation, so to speak. At the same time, it is enriched and made unique by the personality of the Christian. He communicates his translation in a way peculiar to him, and since no two people are alike,

[2] Fred G. Holloway, *New Testament Foundations for Christian Evangelism* (Nashville: Tidings, 1965), p. 13.

the characteristics of the witnessing Christian must be seen as variable and flexible.

Because this unique quality of the witnessing process is often creative and powerful, I shall return to it later in the chapter, but here, for illustrative purposes, I would like to recognize samples of life styles which other writers have outlined as characteristic of the Christian person. To do this I shall turn to the great Christian classic *Imitation of Christ* and then in contrast to a modern attempt made by one of the death-of-God theologians, William Hamilton, in his book *The New Essence of Christianity*.

Imitation of Christ is precisely what its title implies: it is a handbook to show how the individual Christian ought to think and act if he patterns his life after Jesus Christ. Though we do not know for certain who authored this devotional classic, Thomas à Kempis, an Augustinian monk, is often given credit for it. The book was first issued in 1441, and since then over a thousand editions have appeared.

To illustrate the nature of this attempt to describe characteristics of the mature Christian, I shall randomly select a few excerpts from the edition which appears before me on my desk:

Whosoever then would fully and feelingly understand the words of Christ, must endeam to conform his life wholly to the life of Christ.[3]

[3] Thomas à Kempis, *Imitation of Christ* (Philadelphia: Henry Altemus, 1894), p. 22.

143

When a man humbleth himself for his failing, then he easily pacifieth others, and quickly satisfieth those that are offended with him.[4]

Above all things, and in all things, O my soul, thou shalt rest in the Lord always, for he himself is the everlasting rest of the saints.

Grant me, O most sweet and loving Jesus, to rest in thee, above all creatures, above all health and beauty, above all glory and honor, above all power and dignity, above all knowledge and subtilty, above all riches and arts, above all joy and gladness, above all fame and praise, above all sweetness and comfort, above all hope and promise, above all desert and desire:

Above all gifts and benefits that thou canst give and impart upon us, above all mirth and joy that the mind of man can receive and feel:

Finally, above angels and archangels, and above all the heavenly hosts, above all things visible and invisible, and above all that thou art not, O my God.[5]

These excerpts give us a taste of how this Augustinian monk found his life in Christ. Undoubtedly, the *Imitation of Christ* has served as a spiritual compass for millions of devout Christians; perhaps only the Bible has surpassed it in importance.

But now let's jump six centuries and note what a contemporary Christian has to say about the life style of the Christian. William Hamilton ends his little

[4] *Ibid.*, p. 73.
[5] *Ibid.*, pp. 145-46.

book *The New Essence of Christianity* in an attempt to outline a style of life especially appropriate for Christians in modern times. By the phrase "style of life" Hamilton refers to the way the Christian faith is lived out, both in its personal as well as its social context. The contents of this style of life include the following items:

1. *A sense of reserve or reticence in our dealings with others.*
2. *A combination of tolerance and anger.*
3. *"Renounce . . . every hope or wish for more than toleration."*
4. *A recovery of goodness.*

Such characteristics, argues Hamilton, are part of a Christian style of life for modern times.

Certainly these two illustrations, even in such terribly sketchy form, can help us see the difficulty of making specific the ways the Christian gospel is to be personified. The individual Christian's witness is *his*, and this means that he will need to work it out for himself under the guidance of the Holy Spirit. Of course, he can and ought to seek the help of others, including the Bible, Augustinian monks, radical theologians, and so forth. But in the end he confronts contemporary atheism with the gospel as it has been translated through his life.

Perhaps the best general advice St. Augustine gave on this point was, "Love God and do as you please." A bit more specific is Duchesne's often quoted advice: "Work away in utter sincerity and open-mindedness; lead as deep and devoted a spiritual life as you can; renounce, from the first and every day, every hope or wish for more than toleration; and then, with those three activities and dispositions, trust and wait, with indomitable patience and humility, to be tolerated and excused." [6]

This is perhaps the most we can do in the witness of our faith. Whether it is enough to answer the claims of contemporary atheism, we do not know for the simple reason that the Christian community has not seriously tested this approach.

ATHEISM AS AN AID TO THE CHRISTIAN

In the attempt to meet modern atheism as individual Christians we will need the help of all the resources available within the community of the faithful. We will seek help from the Bible, and we will hope for the support of the Christian fellowship, including the church. Prayer, worship, and all those resources which are unique to our faith will also be needed.

But we will also need to draw on the very forces which confront us with their claims of unbelief. Atheism in all its forms can prove to be a positive force in the individual Christian's life if he will consider it in the context of humility and patience.

[6] Quoted in Friedrich von Hügel, *Spiritual Counsel and Letters*, Douglas V. Steere, ed. (New York: Harper & Row, 1964), pp. 46-47.

This book began with a plea for an honest attempt to understand atheism. As Christians facing contemporary unbelief, our first obligation is to accept it as a genuine world view, as a thought and feeling system designed to find meaning in the world of here and now. The Christian must not dismiss or minimize the fact of unbelief. Instead, in humility and patience we must open ourselves to its arguments and claims, considering all we hear and see within the context of our own faith.

But this openness is not enough. We must also listen carefully and prayerfully to the criticism of the atheists, for this is where we can learn much about our faith and about ourselves.

We will learn first of all that atheism can be a crucial test of faith. It has never been easy to believe when others—perhaps even those we admire because of their intellectual skills—practice unbelief. Nor has it been easy to witness to our faith without appearing shallow and sanctimonious. Yet the Christian is called to witness, even if he be misunderstood.

After all, atheism, no matter what its type, can sear away the barnacles of superstition and apathy, if we do not withdraw from it. We must stand our ground, forever knowing that faith, when all is said and done, is simply casting our lot on one side of an adventure rather than on the other side. Of course, casting one's lot ought not to be taken lightly, but it does reduce itself to this when argumentation is exhausted and one stands alone in the need to decide.

At such times—and such times come often to the Christian open to the world and its claims—the individual Christian would do well to listen diligently to the claims of the unbeliever. He might hear the real power of the questions of evil and suffering calling him to struggle with the age-old dilemma of a good God and a suffering world. And he might learn to know that *service* to his fellowman becomes the test of his faith, the claim that is put on him by both the faithful and the unfaithful.

Atheism may also help us to sense when our faith has hung itself up on a false God. The individual Christian is not exempt from idolatry; in fact, he is often especially prone toward it. After all, faith is always the faith of a particular person who feels, thinks, and acts, and who must have some image or likeness of God to round out his life. He is often tempted amid his spiritual quest to reject the world and its values or to embrace it and give it a divine status. In such circumstances atheism can be a positive corrective in that it may cause a man to let go his fanatic hold on false gods. The ancient gods and fate have always threatened wholesome belief in a living God, and in this sense atheism and its arguments can correct man from falling beneath the weight of fate and the idols which storm in upon him.

Atheism can remind us, often in painful but clear ways, that our faith is in continuous need of examination and purgation. The individual Christian needs

148

to have his faith on the firing line or it will become flabby and apathetic. The atheists can serve as wholesome catalysts if we keep our ears and hearts open to their claims.

The Christian's answer to atheism is, then, the witness of his own life. Anything less than this will not be up to the serious claims of modern atheism. Put simply, every Christian is called to be a saint—not a pietistic and withdrawn shadow, but a man in Christ in this world.

A COMMON GROUND

But witnessing before atheists to the conviction that God lives requires a common ground. To communicate effectively we must come to a place where the individual atheist can meet with the individual Christian. Such a meeting is not likely to take place in the church basement, nor is there much chance that it will form on the debate platform, except perhaps in a cruel and ineffective way.

Where, then, can the Christian and the atheist meet? There may be many areas where both can face one another in open dialogue. But I should like to suggest that it is in the acts of service that both can come together in a meaningful way.

In describing the time close to the end of Christ's life, Edwin Prince Booth shows Jesus talking with his disciples. "They talk over their situation and all about the Kingdom," he writes. "Still the simple

149

questions of authority and thrones, still the quiet answers of service and obedience. In proper custom Jesus, as host, washes the feet of his disciples, unsandalled and dusty, and makes of it a lesson on the character of the Kingdom's citizens: service." [7]

This, I believe, is the key. For as we have seen, many contemporary atheists find the support of their unbelief in the sufferings of the world. Even the Christian atheist frequently cries out against the evils of the world.

Both know that there is much good to be done. No one can deny this. And, after all, what makes Christianity is not belief but belief in action. The Christian is called into the world, and he is compelled to do good works. He knows that good works alone are not enough, but good works alone may be enough to meet unbelief. That the Christian does his good works to glorify God, and the atheist to glorify man is a point which will come to be resolved at a later time, if indeed it needs resolution. Now, however, both meet the needs of a struggling world and this gives them the solid ground on which they can confront one another.

I know that there will be those who would rather argue theology and theory. There will be those who will wish to quote Marx or Lenin. Some will find arguing over the death of God more exciting. Many will see no need or contest, blinded by their own

[7] Edwin Prince Booth, *One Sovereign Life* (Nashville: Abingdon Press, 1965), pp. 124-25.

personal and emotional needs. Yet all of these cannot deny for long those who in the name of a living God heal the sick, feed the hungry, educate the ignorant, clothe the naked, and shed light where there is darkness.

SUMMARY

The individual Christian's answer to contemporary atheism may be found in the nature of the gospel itself. The core of the gospel is action, people at work in the world, people who claim that the good they do is done through the grace of a loving, living God. Once the theology of the gospel becomes the psychology of persons, the incarnation is manifested in concrete acts of love and devotion.

The particular ways the gospel is shown in the lives of individuals are difficult to describe because each life is in itself different. Even to imitate Christ introduces the creative uniqueness of personhood and makes such an attempt variable. A Christian life style is essential, but it cannot be put down in a precise fashion. There are no carbon copy Christians.

Individual Christians will meet modern atheism with all the resources available to them, and they will find added help in unbelief itself, for atheism can cleanse corroding faith and purify a faith which tends to become infected with idols and self-righteousness.

Though there may be many points at which the

151

atheist and Christian can meet in open confrontation, the area of service to one's fellowmen represents one which ought to appeal to the genuine believer and unbeliever alike. At least service provides a starting point where an adventure in the search for meaning can fruitfully begin.

INDEX